GREAT DOCTRINES OF THE BIBLE

W.A.Criswell

GREAT DOCTRINES OF THE BIBLE

Volume 3 • Ecclesiology

Edited by
Paige Patterson, President
Criswell Center for Biblical Studies

ZONDERVAN
PUBLISHING HOUSE   OF THE ZONDERVAN CORPORATION
GRAND RAPIDS, MICHIGAN 49506

GREAT DOCTRINES OF THE BIBLE, Volume 3
Copyright © 1983 by The Zondervan Corporation
Grand Rapids, Michigan

Library of Congress Cataloging in Publication Data
(Revised for volume 3)

Criswell, W. A. (Wallie A.), 1909–
    Great doctrines of the Bible.

    1. Baptists—Sermons. 2. Southern Baptist convention—Sermons. 3. Sermons, American. I. Patterson, Paige. II. Title.

BX6333.C77G7   1982   252'.06132   81-16334
ISBN 0-310-43900-0

Edited by Paige Patterson

Printed in the United States of America

83 84 85 86 87 88 89 /10 9 8 7 6 5 4 3 2 1

Dedication

The preparation of the sermon series on the *Great Doctrines of the Bible* has been arduous and time-consuming. The task, however, has been greatly facilitated through the coming of Dr. Tom Melzoni to assist the pastor in the administration of our dear church. Therefore, to my fellow elder Dr. Tom Melzoni, and his helpmeet Trina, I dedicate this volume of sermons on Ecclesiology.

Contents

Foreword

This series of doctrinal sermons represents the climax of many years of preaching and writing. I have given more hours in research and more time to study and meditation in the preparation of these messages than to any other series I have presented in my more than fifty years of preaching. It is my earnest prayer that all of these volumes will provide for the reader a clear understanding of the truths of Scripture concerning the great doctrines of our faith. They are presented in these pages, not as professional, academic lectures in a classroom, but as an appeal for souls from a pulpit to a living congregation.

Many have assisted me in the project. Certainly I am deeply indebted to the president of our Center for Biblical Studies, Dr. Paige Patterson. This gifted and learned theologian assumed the responsibility for overseeing the task of editing these many sermons that will extend over a several-year period of pulpit ministry. The typists for this project are the very efficient and capable Jo Ellen Burch and Marla Hanks, and the stylistic editing has been done by Dr. Dorothy Patterson. Then, last but not least, I owe a debt of gratitude to the layman in our great church who made the project possible by providing equipment and secretary. He insists on remaining anonymous to you, but God has recorded his deed of kindness.

W. A. Criswell
Pastor's Study
First Baptist Church
Dallas, Texas

Introduction

This volume contains no ivory-tower theology. The research has been as thorough as if the author wished to present an erudite, multivolume *Magnum Opus*. Then the research was laid before the One whose eyes are "like a flame or fire" until cold insights were warmed into white-hot convictions of the soul in prayer before God.

Then twice each Lord's Day morning, Dr. W. A. Criswell approached the sacred desk in the auditorium of the First Baptist Church in Dallas, Texas, where he has served as pastor for thirty-eight years. Three thousand people, a standing-room-only crowd, lined the holy place in the heart of one of America's great cities, and listened intently as the investigations, experiences, and convictions of a fifty-year ministry resounded throughout the sanctuary.

Nor were these concepts laboriously deposited in the minds of hearers gathered for the purpose of curing the most hopeless insomniac. Those of us who attended each Sunday went like "empty pitchers to a full fountain." We listened to profound truths depicted in picturesque language, cogently illustrated, and delivered with the fiery oratorical excellence that has characterized our pastor from his youth. We laughed, wept, confessed, expressed thanksgiving, and marched out to engage the enemy.

Each volume of doctrinal sermons represents theology propounded where it ought to be—in the congregations of the Lord. The second volume was devoted to the doctrines of Theology

11

proper and Christology. The present volume examines the crucial doctrine of Ecclesiology, a doctrine that has been the heartbeat of the Free Church people since the dawn of their movement in the Zurich study of Zwingli in 1523. The coalescence of academic theory and practical theology is nowhere better observed in the writings of Dr. Criswell than in these sermons. The skilled theologian and the sensitive pastor are wed together.

We wish to express our special gratitude to Dr. Criswell's friend of many years, Mr. Pat Zondervan, who encouraged the pastor to produce sermonically his mature theological reflection.

In the hope that it will bless the Christian world as greatly as it has blessed our dear church, we humbly present Dr. W. A. Criswell's sermons on the great doctrines of the faith.

Paige Patterson, President
Criswell Center for Biblical Studies

GREAT DOCTRINES OF THE BIBLE

1

The Church Jesus Built

And I say also unto thee, That thou art Peter [*petros,* meaning a "small throwable stone"], and upon this rock [*petra,* an "immovable ledge of rock" upon which you could build a city] I will build my church; and the gates of hell shall not prevail against it (Matt. 16:18).

The word translated "the gates of hell" literally means "death." *Katischuō* is translated "shall not prevail against it." *Katō* means "down" or "against," and *eschuō* means "to have strength and power." Jesus is saying "I will build my church, and death, fire, flood, martyrdom, and blood shall not be able to keep it down. It shall rise and live forever."

All other institutions in our world are eventually buried in death—whether they are political, economic, or social. All other relationships we make in life are finally dissolved in death. A king is no longer a king in the grave. A corporate magnate is no longer a tycoon in the grave. A Hollywood or Broadway star is no longer a star in the grave. But the relationships we make in the church abide and live forever.

I read of a New Testament that was washed ashore on a southern Pacific island. The native found it, read it, and organized a New Testament church according to the instruction in that New Testament. The church, the institution that Christ loved and for whom He died, is vibrant and living, not because of a self-chosen name nor because of a certain kind of history; rather, the church that Jesus built lives forever because it is characterized by five fundamental, foundational articles of faith and practice.

Here are those five enduring characteristics of the church that Jesus built:

THE HOLY SCRIPTURE IS THE
ONLY RULE OF FAITH AND PRACTICE

The church lives in its description and organization by and through and upon the Word of God. Jesus said to His disciples,

> . . . These are the words which I spake unto you, while I was yet with you, that all things must be fulfilled, which were written in the law [*Torah*] of Moses, and in the prophets [*nebiim*], and in the psalms [*kethubim*], concerning me.
>
> Then opened he their understanding, that they might understand the scriptures,
>
> And said unto them, Thus it is written, and thus it behooved Christ to suffer, and to rise from the dead the third day:
>
> And that repentance and remission of sins should be preached in his name among all nations, beginning at Jerusalem.
>
> And ye are witnesses of these things (Luke 24:44–48).

The Scriptures tell us that Christ was born; He lived; He died; He was buried. According to those same Scriptures, He was raised from the dead; He is at the right hand of God as our Great Intermediary and High Priest. Those same Scriptures tell us He is coming again to rapture the church to Himself and to provide for us who make up the church a home with Him in heaven world without end. Christ lived, died, taught, and built His church. That church abiding forever lives according to the immutable, unchanging word of God.

In the days of the apostles, the church lived by the oral teaching of the apostles.

> And they continued steadfastly in the apostles' doctrine and fellowship, and in breaking of bread, and in prayers (Acts 2:42).

Here the "apostles' doctrine" refers to the oral teaching *(didachē)*. The first three books of the New Testament are called the synoptic Gospels because much of their content is the same or similar. That common material was the oral teaching of the apostles.

When the apostles died, God had this oral teaching written down, and it became the teaching (*didachē*) of the apostles—an important part of our New Testament. The church is built upon that great doctrinal revelation of God.

In our Lord's ministry, He appealed to the Scriptures. In John 5:39 He said, "Search the scriptures." The apostles did this in Berea, ". . . and searched the scriptures daily, whether those things were so" (Acts 17:11). Thus it is that the Word of God gives life, birth, and direction to the family of God, and the church is built upon that commitment.

In the days of the Reformation, after the church had drifted away from its foundational concept and commitment to the Holy Scripture, Martin Luther and his fellow reformers came forward with a flaming aegis, *sola Scriptura*—"Scripture alone"—and that is the foundation of the church that Jesus built.

Every Believer Is a Priest

> And, behold, the veil of the temple was rent in twain from the top to the bottom [not from the bottom to the top, as though men had done it, but from the top to the bottom because God did it]; and the earth did quake, and the rocks rent (Matt. 27:51).

When that veil was severed, the inner sanctuary, the dwelling place of God, was open to view and access. There Isaiah saw Him in that very place, high and lifted up. There the high priest entered with the blood of atonement once a year. There he made intercession in behalf of the people.

Now, however, that veil of separation is forever destroyed. It hangs as limp as a useless rag. Anyone now has full access to God without the mediation of a priest or sacerdotal representative. He can come to God for himself, and he can talk to God face to face as a man would to his friend. He can call upon the name of the Lord from a kitchen corner as well as from a gilded cathedral. Any man can stand before God as his own priest and offer sacrifices of witness, praise, and testimony to the Lord. It is a glorious thing God has done for us, and the priesthood of the believer is the second great foundational stone upon which our Lord has built His church. Every man has a right to talk to God for himself and to listen to the voice of the Lord in his own heart and soul without an officiating, sacerdotal system to intervene.

The Church Is a Congregation

The church is a regenerated, "born-again" congregation of the Lord's people.

> Then Peter said unto them, Repent, and be baptized every one of you in the name of Jesus Christ for [*eis*, meaning "because of"—because of what Christ has done for us] the remission of sins, and ye shall receive the gift of the Holy Ghost.
>
> Then they that gladly received his word were baptized: and the same day there were added unto them about three thousand souls.
>
> And they continued steadfastly in the apostles' doctrine [*didachē*, the oral teaching that was later written down in what we call the New Testament] and fellowship [*koinonia*], and in breaking of bread [the Lord's Supper, which is the continuing church ordinance], and in prayers (Acts 2:38, 41–42).

The church is a born-again fellowship. The word in the New Testament is *ekklēsia*, meaning "that which is called out." It is a called-out body, the elect unto God. In the beginning, God elected the man above all the sentient animals around him. God elected Noah above all other antediluvians. He elected Abraham out of a world of idolatry. He elected Israel (Jacob) over Edom (Esau). He elected Judah from among his brethren. He elected David from among the families of Judah. He elected Bethlehem from among the cities of Israel. He elected Mary from among the daughters of the family of the Lord. He elected the apostles from among the followers of Christ. He elected Paul to be His emissary to the Gentiles. He has elected you and me. He has called us to be a part of the *ekklēsia*, the "called-out" family of the Lord, and to be separated from the world.

By no means is the church congruous with the state. By natural birth we are born citizens of the state, but we must be "reborn" to be a member of the family of God and of the church of Jesus Christ. We are born naturally into the state, but we must be born again supernaturally into the family of God. The church is the convocation, the gathering together of these regenerated members who have been called into faith and into the family of the Lord.

The Church Has a Twofold Order and Ordinance

The church has a twofold order of ordained ministers and a twofold ordinance to be observed faithfully by its members. When Paul speaks of this in writing to the church in Philippi, he mentions bishops and deacons—only those two.

> Paul and Timothy, the servants of Jesus Christ, to all the saints in Christ Jesus which are at Philippi, with the bishops and deacons (Phil. 1:1).

There are two orders of ordination in the church. The first one is the bishop, for which three words are used in the New Testament. He is called a *presbuteros,* translated "elder," referring to the dignity of his office; he is called an *episkopos,* translated "bishop" and meaning "overseer," referring to his assignment; he is called a *poimēn*, meaning "shepherd," "pastor"—one who has love in his heart for the people, and one who intercedes and cares for them. All three of these words are used interchangeably in the New Testament to describe the first ordained officer of the church Jesus built.

There is one other office—the deacon. In Paul's day the Greek word *diakonos* was a household word meaning "servant." The deacons were men who were set aside and consecrated to hold up the hands of the pastor. As Hur and Aaron held up the hands of Moses, so the deacons of our generation are set aside to hold up the hands of the pastor. When pastor and deacon work together in the spirit of Christ, they comprise an unbeatable team—the preacher and his laymen.

There are also two ordinances. They are not sacraments; they are not the means for salvation or grace. Rather, they portray the gospel. Like a dipper holds and shapes the water, the two great ordinances that Christ gave His church hold and shape the truth. If there is a departure or aberration from them, its repercussion is felt throughout the doctrinal structure of the entire body.

The initial ordinance of baptism is a dramatic picture of the gospel and our experience in it. Paul defined the gospel in his letter to the Corinthians.

> Moreover, brethren, I declare unto you the gospel which I preached unto you, which also ye have received, and wherein ye stand;
> By which also ye are saved, if ye keep in memory what I preached unto you, unless ye have believed in vain.
> For I delivered unto you first of all that which I also received, how that Christ died for our sins according to the scriptures;
> And that he was buried, and that he rose again the third day according to the scriptures (I Cor. 15:1-4).

That ordinance portrays the fact that we are dead with Christ, buried with Him, and then raised with Him to walk in a new life.

The recurring church ordinance is the Lord's Supper. "This do in remembrance of me." This ordinance looks back to the day when our Lord suffered for our sins, and it looks forward to the day when He is coming again. The broken bread presents His torn and mangled body, and the crimson of the cup represents the red blood of His life poured out for us. The church that Jesus built is characterized by two orders and by two ordinances.

THE CHURCH HAS A BINDING COMMISSION

The fifth tremendous foundational article of faith in the church is its abiding commission. The Gospel of Matthew closes with these words:

> And Jesus came and spake unto them, saying, All power is given unto me in heaven and in earth.
> Go ye therefore, and teach [*mathēteuō*] all nations, baptizing [*baptizō*] them in the name of the Father, and of the Son, and of the Holy Ghost: Teaching [*didaskō*] them to observe all things whatsoever I have commanded you: and, lo, I am with you alway, even unto the end of the world (Matt. 28:18–20).

Our tremendous assignment and commission to the end of the earth is threefold: (1) *Mathēteuō*—"to make disciples," "to evangelize," "to win to Christ"; (2) *Baptizō*—"to baptize believers in the name of the triune God"; (3) *Didaskō*—to teach them to observe all the things" God has commanded.

The church that Jesus built is characterized by these five fundamental articles of faith: (1) the Bible—the sole rule and foundation for faith in Christ; (2) the priesthood of every believer—the right of any man to approach God for himself; (3) a regenerate church membership of born-again believers, making up the family of God; (4) the twofold order of bishops and deacons and the two ordinances of baptism and the Lord's Supper; (5) the Great Commission, that sets our face toward the conversion and the discipling of the whole earth.

Even as there are five great foundational and constitutional principles upon which Christ built His church, there are many habits, bylaws, and practices of that family of God.

> Not forsaking the assembling of ourselves together, as the manner of some is; but exhorting one another: and so much the more, as ye see the day approaching (Heb. 10:25).

One of the beautiful customs of that first church was to meet together on the Lord's Day. Not by way of commandment, but out of love and deference and remembrance of what Jesus means to us, we come together in God's house.

Jack Hamm, a tremendously gifted Christian artist and a deacon in our beloved church, brought to my study a beautiful picture illustrating this marvelous verse:

> One thing have I desired of the LORD, that will I seek after; that I may dwell in the house of the LORD all the days of my life, to behold the beauty of the LORD, and to inquire in his temple (Ps. 27:4).

The psalmist is simply pleading, "Let me be a part of the family of God and meet with them in the Lord's house."

Meeting in the Lord's house has never been coersive duty for me. Even as a child, I loved to go to the little white crackerbox of a church where I was converted and baptized. I loved it then, and I love it today. I would rather come to church than go any-where in the world. I love God's people. I love to listen to the orchestra play and to hear the choir sing. I love to see the people. If I could, I would like to stand somewhere and shake hands and say a word of encouragement to everybody who ever comes to the house of the Lord.

In Martin Luther's New Testament, which he translated from Greek into German, he characteristically used the term *die gemeinde* rather than the word "church" *(kirche)* in translating *ekklēsia*. He picked up a term used for fellowship and commun-ion among the people, on the streets, out in the world where men congregate and fellowship. In the New Testament, it is *koinonia*, "fellowship." That is what the church is: it is a fellowship; it is a communion.

Paul closes his letter to the church at Thessalonica with this admonition.

> Finally, brethren, pray for us, that the word of the Lord may have free course, and be glorified, even as it is with you (2 Thess. 3:1).

Spurgeon, the great London preacher, said to a friend one day, "Friend, someday when you have the ear of the Great King, call my name, pray for me." That is one of the sweetest things I have ever heard.

In his first letter to the Thessalonians, Paul exhorts the breth-ren to

Pray without ceasing.
In every thing give thanks: for this is the will of God in Christ Jesus concerning you (1 Thess. 5:17–18).

That describes the church, the fellowship. We pray for one another, and we love one another. If the church reflects the spirit of Jesus, there is always that sweet fellowship and warm remembrance, "God be good to you; God be good to us," as we encourage each other in the faith, as we lift up each other, bless each other, and love each other.

> . . . and upon this rock I will build my church; and the gates of hell shall not prevail against it (Matt. 16:18).

The church is the body of Christ bound in fellowship and communion forever. I wrote this poem about God's church.

Empire and kingdom, archduke and prince
Are buried beneath the sod.
All that remains of earth's vast domain
Is the church of the living God.

History has finished its slow-moving course.
Fallen are scepter and rod.
All that abides of times and of tides
Is the church of the living God.

Alas for a world steeped in sin and in shame.
Sinking down in despair with a sob;
A world facing fate of repentance too late
To enter the church of God.

Gone are the lusts of the flesh and the heart,
And the passions that sway the mob.
Naught in their place is there ought but to face
The judgment of Almighty God.

Sorrow of sorrows, oh, loss of all losses
The soul of its Savior to rob.
Turning away from Him who could stay
The wrath of Almighty God.

Soon life will be over, soon day will be ended,
Soon flowers and trees cease to nod,
In an earth filled with death,
Where the spirit of breath
Has been taken back unto God.

O stranger in sin; O child without hope,
O wearied of earth's ways to plod.
Forsake evil night, come into Christ's light
And rest in the fold of God.

Why would a man choose to go through life and separate himself from the sweet and precious fellowship of the Lord and His people? Why would a man come to the end of the way and face the darkness of night and despair, of judgment and death when God opens the door, tears asunder the veil that separates us, and bids us to enter full, free, and welcome?

> Let us therefore come boldly unto the throne of grace, that we may obtain mercy, and find grace to help in time of need (Heb. 4:16).

This God has done for us. Welcome, sweet friend, into the fellowship, into the *koinonia*, into the *gemeinde*, into the communion of God's sweet fellowship.

2

The Church
the Holy Spirit Quickened

> Then they that gladly received his word were baptized: and the same day there were added unto them about three thousand souls.
> And they continued steadfastly in the apostles' doctrine and fellowship, and in breaking of bread, and in prayers (Acts 2:41–42).

The church is the work of the gracious and omnipotent hands of Jesus Himself. On the day of Pentecost, as described in Acts 2, the church was empowered and quickened.

Before Pentecost the church that Jesus built had twenty-seven characteristic features:

1. Christian believers had the gospel (Mark 1:1).
2. They were converted.
3. They were baptized after conversion.
4. They had Christ as their head.
5. They were instructed in church truths.
6. They were called to obey Christ.
7. Some were ordained.
8. They were commissioned.
9. They were organized for their needs.
10. They had a missionary program.
11. They had a teaching program.
12. They had a healing program.
13. They were promised a continuing and permanent congregation (Matt. 16:18).
14. They had church discipline.
15. They had divine authority.

16. They had the essentials of church life.
17. They had a true democracy.
18. They had qualified pastors.
19. They had the Lord's Supper.
20. They had the Holy Spirit (Luke 11:13).
21. They had divine powers to do Christ's work.
22. They had music "in the midst of the church" (Heb. 2:12).
23. They had prayer meetings.
24. They had business meetings.
25. They had a membership roll.
26. They were united and "added unto" their numbers (Acts 2:1, 41).
27. They had Christ as their cornerstone.

All of that existed before the second chapter of the Book of Acts was inspired and written. Christ built the church before the day of Pentecost came.

This building of the church was as the creation of Adam. Genesis 2 says that the Lord formed Adam out of the dust of the ground and that he lay there inert before the Lord. He was fully formed and fashioned. All of his organs and faculties were in place. The Scripture says,

> And the LORD God formed man of the dust of the ground, and breathed into his nostrils the breath of life; and man became a living soul (Gen. 2:7).

Even so Christ formed the church, and at Pentecost the Holy Spirit breathed life and quickening power into it.

We see another brilliant example of that quickening in Ezekiel 37. The prophet sees a valley filled with dry bones, and he is commanded to prophesy and preach to these bones. When he does so, the bones come together in skeletal form. As he continues to prophesy, those bones are covered with sinews and muscles. Then the Lord God tells the prophet to call down the breath of the Lord, and the breath of the Lord enters those bones so that they arise as a great, living army for God.

In this way Christ formed, organized, and built the church, and at Pentecost the Holy Spirit of God inbreathed, empowered, quickened, and awakened the church of the living God so that it became a vibrant and living body.

Acts 2 contains a description of that living, quickened church.

> And they continued steadfastly in the apostles' doctrine and fellowship, and in breaking of bread, and in prayers (Acts 2:42).

In Revelation 21 we read that John sees the church as a perfect cube. The length, height, and breadth of it are equal. It is called the city "foursquare."

This description of the church that was quickened by the Holy Spirit of God has four essential characteristics of that God-empowered, Christ-honoring, and Spirit-filled congregation: the doctrine, the fellowship, the breaking of bread, and the prayers.

THE DOCTRINE OF THE APOSTLES

> And they continued steadfastly in the apostles' doctrine [*didache*, meaning "teaching"] . . . (Acts 2:42).

There is an unbroken succession in the revelation of the truth of God. The apostles and the first generation of believers who receive from their hands that deposit of truth taught the next generation, and that generation taught the following generation until finally the teaching *(didache)*, i.e., the doctrinal truth of God, has come down to us. We are praying that we shall hand that deposit of truth to those who succeed us and that they, in turn, will continue its unbroken succession until the Lord comes again.

These early Christians continued in the spirit, the doctrine, the teaching, and the dedication of the apostles—an unbroken succession through the centuries. It is a real fellowship of the people of the Lord in the truth of God.

On the Mount of Transfiguration, Moses and Elijah spoke with Jesus about the great doctrine of His atoning death. These men lived in times divided by centruies, but the succession of truth from one to the other was unbroken.

In Hebrews 11 are listed the heroes of the faith. The division between chapters 11 and 12 is manmade, for the text should not be divided at this point. In the first verse of chapter 12 after the author of Hebrews has presented the rollcall of heroes of the faith, he says,

> Wherefore seeing we also are compassed about with so great a cloud of witnesses, let us lay aside every weight, and the sin which

doth so easily beset us, and let us run with patience the race that is set before us.

We are in a great unbroken succession of those who have witnessed to the truth of God. I feel it every time I stand in the sacred place of proclamation in the First Baptist Church. Mighty men of God have also stood behind this very pulpit, and we have received from their hands the truth of Almighty God, and pray that the Lord will find those of us who follow, faithful in our handing down of the precious truth. It is this truth, a deposit of the faith, that is the genuine heart and dynamic center of the assembly of God's people.

"They continued *steadfastly* in the apostles' doctrine." The apostles never wearied of teaching the doctrine, and the listeners never tired of hearing it. The truth of God is never dull, dreary, dry, or monotonous—not unless you are a mere spectator who has not allowed the great truth of God to become a vibrant, living part of your life.

A dear young woman who once belonged to my congregation was anxious that her husband come and be with us. After she spoke to me about it, I visited her husband and urged him to be a part of our church, along with his wife.

As I pressed the appeal, he finally said to me, "Would you like to know why I do not want to join your church?"

I made the mistake of saying, "Yes, why?"

He said, "I will not join your church because I do not like to hear you preach."

Well, in my most kind and generous way, I thanked him for his candid observation. Then, out of curiosity I said, "I would like to know why you do not like to hear me preach. It seems to me that everybody would like to hear me preach."

He said, "I have been down there several times with my wife, and every time I go you preach the Bible. I have never heard you preach anything else."

I responded, "You are right. What do you want me to preach?"

The man continued, "When I go to church, I would like the minister to enlarge my field of interest, expounding on the political scene, on our economic dilemma, on current events, or about the latest and finest literature. I get tired of listening to you just preach the Bible."

I never won him, and he never joined the church because I never quit preaching the Bible, but I turned that discussion over and over in my mind.

I would like to have you answer me honestly. Does television talk about the news of the day? Do magazines like *Newsweek, Time, U.S. News & World Report* discuss the economic life of the people, the current events, the state of the nation, the political scene? Does the daily newspaper in its headlines, features, and editorials discuss the events of the day? Why would you want to come to church and hear all of that rehashed?

Every man in the State Department knows more about the inside working of American foreign policy than I could ever know. It seems to me that once in awhile a man who lives in the present world would like to know what God has to say. If God does say anything, who else but the preacher—God's spokesman —will tell us what God says! I am convinced that this is the assignment of the preacher—to stand in the pulpit, to open the Word of the living Lord, and to tell us how our souls can be saved and how we can enjoy the blessings of God in our lives.

The Fellowship of Believers

Will you look again at this full-orbed outpouring of the Spirit of God and its effect upon the church? "And they continued steadfastly in . . . fellowship" (*koinōnia*). In 1 Corinthians 10, *koinōnia* is translated "communion." We have communion when we break bread and drink the cup together; we experience fellowship in the Lord.

From the beginning of time, God's eternal purpose has been for His people to be together. "God setteth the solitary in families . . ." (Ps. 68:6). All of us are in some kind of family. That family may suffer from disorder, disorganization, and destruction, but everyone is born into some kind of a family group. And, of course, how much more should we be together in the church, which is the family of God.

A preacher was once surrounded by unbelievers. One of them said to him, "Preacher, do you believe we can go to heaven without joining the church?"

The preacher immediately replied, "Yes."

They liked that. They patted him on the back and commended him for being such a broadminded preacher.

28

Then the preacher said to them, "May I ask you a question, and will you answer just as quickly?"

They said, "Yes, preacher, what is it?"

He asked, "Why would you want to go to heaven where we are going to praise our Lord forever when you refuse to honor him here? Why would you want to go to heaven to be with God's people for eternity when you scorn their fellowship and ignore their communion here on earth?"

My friend, the sweetest privilege in the world is to belong to the family of God, to the assembly of believers, to the *koinōnia* of the Lord's people. How precious it is! There are thousands of manmade entities—civic, philanthropic, and social organizations. But there is just one that Jesus made. Christ loved the church and gave Himself for it, and we are added to the church by the Spirit of God.

> For by one Spirit are we all baptized into one body [the family of the Lord], whether we be Jews or Gentiles, whether we be bond or free; and have been all made to drink into one Spirit (1 Cor. 12:13).

It is the highest privilege in the world to belong to that family of God. In this world we face a floodtide of secularism and materialism. Our great First Baptist Church is like an island of God's mercy and grace in the vast city of Dallas. It is like a colony of heaven. We gather here with our children, our teenagers, our young married, our men and women in the prime of their lives, and finally with those in old age and near death.

The tribes of Gad and Manasseh on one side of the Jordan were no less a part of Israel than the tribes on the other side of the Jordan. Some are there and others are here, but we all belong to the family of God. This is a special comfort when I see our people come to old age and death. Practically all of the people that I knew when I first came to Dallas many years ago are on the other side. Every leader in the church during my earliest years is over there. It comforts my heart to know we are still one in the faith. Death does not separate us from Christ or from one another. We are in the family of God—the *koinōnia*, the assembly of God's people.

THE BREAKING OF BREAD BY THE FAITHFUL

"And they continued steadfastly in the apostles' doctrine and fellowship, and in breaking of bread. . . ." From my study and understanding of the Scriptures, it seems to me that the earliest Christian community observed the "breaking of bread"—the New Testament phrase alluding to the Lord's Supper—at the close of every evening meal as they broke bread and shared the fruit of the vine together.

> And they, continuing daily with one accord in the temple, and breaking bread from house to house, did eat their meat with gladness and singleness of heart (Acts 2:46).

What is the broken bread? That symbolizes His torn and mangled body. What is the crimson cup? That represents His life as it is poured out on the ground. Therefore, the "breaking of bread" reminds us of the agony and the suffering of our Lord's atoning death on the cross. This memorial is called the *eucharist*—because the word used in its description means "to give thanks" (*eucharisteō*). The Lord took bread, gave thanks, and broke it. He took the cup, gave thanks, and drank it.

It is no wonder that this eucharistic faith shook the very foundations of the Roman Empire. These believers rejoiced in the sufferings, hardships, and trials of life.

"They that gladly received his word were baptized . . ." (Acts 2:41). Verse 46 says, ". . . breaking bread from house to house, did eat their meat with gladness and singleness of heart." Then I turn to Acts 5 and read,

> And they departed from the presence of the council, rejoicing that they were counted worthy to suffer shame for his name (v. 41).

Though bloody and beaten, they were rejoicing that they were counted worthy to suffer for His name. This is eucharistic Christianity—praising God in suffering, agony, and death.

In his second Corinthian letter, Paul writes:

> . . . There was given to me a thorn in the flesh [a physical ailment], the messenger of Satan to buffet me, lest I should be exalted above measure.
>
> For this thing I besought the Lord thrice, that it might depart from me. [Was he blind? Was he crippled?]
>
> And he said unto me, My grace is sufficient for thee: for my strength is made perfect in weakness. Most gladly therefore will I rather glory in my infirmities, that the power of Christ may rest upon me.
>
> Therefore I take pleasure in infirmities, in reproaches, in necessities, in persecutions, in distresses for Christ's sake: for when I am weak, then am I strong (12:7–10).

Eucharistic Christianity praises God for the trials and the torments, the hurts and the tears, the afflictions and the sicknesses, the frustrations and the disappointments in life.

> In every thing give thanks: for this is the will of God in Christ Jesus concerning you (1 Thess. 5:18).

How do you do that? How do you say "Thank You, Lord, for sickness." You have to learn to pray that. How do you express gratitude when you have been crushed and ground into the dust of the earth? You learn more about God in weakness and infirmity, in disappointment and heartache, than you could ever know about God in your own strength or success or achievement. Eucharistic Christianity is unusual. No wonder it changed the world.

THE PRAYERS OF GOD'S PEOPLE

> And they continued steadfastly in the apostles' doctrine [*didachē*] and fellowship [*koinōnia*], and in breaking of bread [eucharistic Christianity], and in prayers (Acts 2:42).

It is easily noted that the phrase "in prayers" refers to a stated, public service of worship and intercession as well as to an individual's private appeal to God.

Every Sunday I invite the visitors to our church to have fellowship with me after the service. Once we had a visitor who said to me, "I am a Baptist and have been all of my life. I cannot tell you how surprised I was to see your people kneel in prayer."

My intent is not to find fault or castigate or criticize any of my fellow Baptist churches, but I do think that this is one of the saddest commentaries that could ever be made about us. It has always seemed to me that when I who am but dust and ashes talk to God, my place is down on my knees and on my face before the great and mighty God. This Spirit-quickened, awakened church in Acts 2 was characterized by their meeting together for stated public prayer.

The prophet Isaiah, speaking for the Lord, said, ". . . mine house shall be called a house in prayer. . ." (Is. 56:7). Holy convocations of Israel gathered before the door of the tabernacle. We, too, should come to God's house to call upon His name, to open our hearts Godward and Christward and heavenward and to pray that the Lord will fill our souls with His grace and mercy.

31

Then we also need that closet prayer, with the door shut, the private prayer which nobody but God hears. "And they continued steadfastly . . . in prayers."

When I attended the Southern Baptist Theological Seminary in Louisville, Kentucky, my Hebrew teacher was John R. Sampey. He was also president of the school. He was one among peers, one of the most interesting men that you could ever know in your life. Everybody called him "Tiglath" because of his great admiration for Tiglath-Pileser, the powerful king of ancient Assyria.

Dr. Sampey went to Missouri to hold a revival meeting with one of the Southern Seminary graduates. When he returned to the campus revived and on fire, he described the revival and the circumstances, which were more marvelous to me than the revival itself, and which brought genuine revival to pass.

The young pastor of that church had said to his wife, "I am going to resign the church and go into secular work. I am not going to be a preacher any longer."

Surely there is not a preacher in this world who has not had his moments of infinite discouragement and heartache. I can remember walking up and down in front of the little church that I pastored years ago and saying to myself, "I am not going to preach any longer, and I am certainly not going to be a pastor. I am going to medical school and become a doctor as my mother wanted me to be." (My grandfather was a doctor and my mother was disappointed when I said I was going to be a preacher instead of a doctor). I was crushed and discouraged at that time, so I know exactly how this young pastor felt.

His wife replied, "All right, but I have one request to make. For a period of time, would you get up an hour earlier each morning and pray?"

Out of deference to his wife, the young pastor said he would do that. Each morning he got up to pray for an hour. He had never prayed for an hour at one time in his life. Five minutes seemed long, and ten minutes was an eternity. He just ran out of anything to pray about. But because he had promised his wife, he stayed with it. As the mornings came and went, he began to pray for his deacons by name, one at a time. Then he began to pray for his Sunday school teachers and departmental superintendents. He called them by name before the Lord. Then he began to pray for the sick, the bereaved, the distressed, and the heartbroken in his congregation. Then he began to pray for the lost in the community.

Dr. Sampey said, "A great revival came to that young man's heart and his life, and out of him it spilled over into the church. I shared in that glorious revival where God visited us and heaven breathed upon us."

God's will for us is to pray for one another, to pray for ourselves, to pray for those who belong to us, to pray for the work of our hands—that is what we must do.

Every time I am given a new Bible, I write a sentence on the fly leaf at the front: "He stands best who kneels most; he stands strongest who kneels weakest; and he stands longest who kneels longest." Victories for God are not won by might or by power or by human genius, but by His Holy Spirit.

3

The Great Mystery of the Church

The Book of Ephesians is an encyclical; it is a general epistle. Though the *Textus Receptus* happened to address its copy of this letter to the church at Ephesus, it is actually written to all the churches and even to us.

> Husbands, love your wives, even as Christ also loved the church, and gave himself for it;
>
> That he might sanctify and cleanse it with the washing of water by the word.
>
> That he might present it to himself a glorious church, not having spot, or wrinkle, or any such thing; but that it should be holy and without blemish.
>
> So ought men to love their wives as their own bodies. He that loveth his wife loveth himself.
>
> For no man ever yet hated his own flesh; but nourisheth and cherisheth it, even as the Lord the church:
>
> For we are members of his body, of his flesh, and of his bones.
>
> For this cause shall a man leave his father and mother, and shall be joined unto his wife, and they two shall be one flesh.
>
> This is a great mystery [*musterion*]: but I speak concerning Christ and the church (Eph. 5:25–32).

To us the word "mystery" signifies a riddle hid in an enigma wrapped up in a conundrum, something we cannot know or understand. It is unfathomable. But to the Greek, the word *musterion*, which is transliterated into English just as it is written in Greek, had no such connotation. Rather, it referred to the mystery religions, like the Elysian mysteries. No one knew those mysteries, i.e., the secret rites, except those who were initiated into the religion.

The Great Mystery of the Church

The New Testament writers used that word *musterion* to describe the elective purposes of God, those secret plans kept in the heart of God until He chose to reveal them to His holy apostles.

For example, Paul writes in 1 Corinthians:

> Let a man so account of us, as of the ministers of Christ, and stewards of the mysteries of God (4:1).

Jesus used the word when He spoke to His apostles in the Book of Matthew.

> ...it is given unto you to know the mysteries of the kingdom of heaven, but to them it is not given (13:11).

When the Jewish nation rejected Christ, the final kingdom was postponed, and that kingdom took the form of a mystery in the hearts of men. No one ever thought or dreamed of such a thing. It was a secret kept in God's heart until He revealed it.

There are many references to the mysteries of God in the Scriptures. The Incarnation is one. Paul writes of it to Timothy.

> And without controversy great is the mystery of godliness: God was manifest in the flesh, justified in the Spirit, seen of angels, preached unto the Gentiles, believed on in the world, received up into glory (1 Tim. 3:16).

Who could ever think of God as being in human form? Yet He was made manifest in the flesh. That is a mystery.

Paul speaks of the tremendous mystery of the rapture of the church.

> Now this I say, brethren, that flesh and blood cannot inherit the kingdom of God; neither doth corruption inherit incorruption.
> Behold, I show you a mystery; We shall not all sleep [There is going to be a generation that shall never see death; rather they shall be raptured or caught up to God in heaven], but we shall all be changed (1 Cor. 15:50–51).

What a marvelous thing! No man ever knew this mystery kept in the heart of God until that day when God Himself revealed it to His holy apostles.

Thus it is that this word is used in describing the church. It is a new creation. It has a form and substance and significance that no man could ever know by searching. The church is not in the Old Testament. Isaiah, Ezekiel, and Daniel did not see it. If you identify the church with Israel, you are going to find the Word of

God so enigmatic and beyond understanding that finally you will just cast it aside as being a piece of ancient literature or an antique relic of an ancient tribe. It has no meaning; you cannot put it together unless you see the dispensational truth of God.

We see that as Paul writes in Ephesians.

> How that by revelation he made known unto me the mystery; (as I wrote before in few words,
> Whereby, when ye read, ye may understand my knowledge in the mystery of Christ)
> Which in other ages was not made known unto the sons of men, as it is now revealed unto his holy apostles and prophets by the Spirit (Eph. 3:3-5).

Now what is the mystery that Paul is here describing? It is the mystery of His new creation—the church.

> That the Gentiles should be fellow heirs, and of the same body, and partakers of his promise in Christ by the gospel (Eph. 3:6).

God elected, selected, chose the Jewish nation as peculiarly His own. But this *musterion*, a secret God kept in His heart until He revealed it, is that there is to be a new body, a new creation, a new election. That new creation is called the church.

Paul writes that the church is given to us.

> And to make all men see what is the fellowship of the mystery, which from the beginning of the world hath been hid in God, who created all things by Jesus Christ:
> To the intent that now unto the principalities and powers in heavenly places might be known by the church the manifold wisdom of God,
> According to the eternal purpose which he purposed in Christ Jesus our Lord (Eph. 3:9-11).

It is a gloriously new and wonderful thing that God has done. In this new creation, the church, there are Jew and Gentile, male and female, bond and free, rich and poor, old and young, educated and uneducated—all together the body of Christ, making up one glorious congregation in the Lord called the church.

A FURTHER REVELATION OF THE MYSTERY OF THE CHURCH

Paul writes of the church in an unusual way in our text. He speaks of the origin of the church.

For we are members of his body, of his flesh, and of his bones.

For this cause shall a man leave his father and mother, and shall be joined unto his wife, and they two shall be one flesh.

This is a great mystery: but I speak concerning Christ and the church (Eph. 5:30–32).

In describing this *musterion*—this new creation—Paul refers to Genesis 2:21–24.

And the LORD God caused a deep sleep to fall upon Adam, and he slept: and he took one of his ribs [*tsela,* meaning "side," like the side of a mountain, the side of the ark, the side of the tabernacle, the side of the golden altar of incense. The word is used all through the Bible, but it is only translated "rib" in this one place.] and closed up the flesh instead thereof;

And the rib, which the LORD God had taken from man, made he a woman, and brought her unto the man.

And Adam said, This is now bone of my bones, and flesh of my flesh: she shall be called Woman, [*ishah*] because she was taken out of Man.

Therefore shall a man leave his father and his mother, and shall cleave unto his wife: and they shall be one flesh.

We see this reference again as Paul wrote in Ephesians.

For this cause shall a man leave his father and mother, and shall be joined unto his wife, and they two shall be one flesh.

This is a great mystery: but I speak concerning Christ and the church (5:31–32).

The apostle says that Eve was taken out of the side of Adam, so the church was taken out of the side of our Lord. We are born out of His sobs and tears, wounds and agony, blood and suffering—out of our Lord's side from which poured the crimson of His life, out of the Savior's sufferings. Who would ever have thought that the church of Jesus Christ would be born out of the Roman government's brutal condemnation and execution of a man. It is a *musterion,* a secret kept in the heart of God until the day He revealed it to His apostles, to the world, and to us.

It is a marvelous and wonderful thing. It was wonderful in its sign or symbol—i.e., in the creation of Eve out of the side of Adam. It is even more wonderful when we see the antitype—the creation of the church out of the sufferings, tears, and cross of our Lord. We are taken from His side, from near His heart.

Paul declares that Christ loved the church. If you are a mother, you can enter into that concept of love beyond what any of us who are fathers can ever understand. In the travail and agony of birth, a mother somehow loves the child in a depth or height that no man could ever quite reach. Having suffered for the child, the mother loves in a way that is deep and unique.

So it is with Christ and His church. Having suffered and died for us, having poured out His life for us, He loves us in a deeper way. Christ loved the church and gave Himself for it. He never said, "My wife." He never said, "My child." But He did say, "My church." Christ loved the church and gave Himself for it.

> For this cause shall a man leave his father and mother, and shall
> be joined unto his wife, and they two shall be one flesh (Eph. 5:31).

We are joined to Christ in one body. Indissolubly, inextricably, and everlastingly, we are one with our Lord. As He is, we are; as we are, He is. We are not to be separated. We are crucified with Him; we are buried with Him; we are raised with Him; we are ascended with Him; we are to be in heaven with Him. He is our head, and we are joined in body to Him. He is with us in this earth. We are His body. We are the voice of Christ to preach the gospel of salvation. We are the heart of Christ in compassionate love and remembrance. Nowhere in the Bible do you find the Lord saying, "Take away these lepers, the crippled, the blind, and the poor." He always said, "Bring them unto me." He healed them all. We are His feet to visit and to bring the message of salvation. We are His hands to help and to serve.

Whenever you expound the word of God truthfully and correctly, all of the parts will beautifully fit together. If you do not expound it correctly, there will be parts of it that are jagged and do not fit. Let me give you an illustration of that.

One of the tremendous doctrines of the Bible is that of election, predestination, or the everlasting security of the saints in salvation. In heaven God has a book in which He has written the names of those who have been saved. Every one of them will answer to His name in that ultimate and final day. Not one will be lost.

> And I give unto them eternal life; and they shall never perish,
> neither shall any man pluck them out of my hand (John 10:28).

When you preach that doctrine of election or predestination faithfully, revealing that the omnipotent choice and power of God is for those who find refuge in Him to be saved and saved forever, every little part of the Bible will fit together beautifully, accurately, and perfectly. Here is an instance of that.

> Now ye are the body of Christ, and members in particular (1 Cor. 12:27).

Paul avows that all of us are members of the body of Christ, having been baptized into His body by the Holy Spirit.

> For by one Spirit are we all baptized into one body, whether we be Jews or Gentiles, whether we be bond or free; and have been all made to drink into one Spirit (1 Cor. 12:13).

Then Paul continues to talk about the different members of that body. He refers to the hand, foot, eye, and ear. When you preach the doctrine of the eternal security of God's people it fits, for it would be a doctrine alien to the Scriptures to say that God adds a hand to His body and then chops it off and finally puts it back on again. To be saved, lost, saved again, then lost again would be like putting your hand on, cutting it off, and putting it back on again. When God adds a foot or a hand or an eye to His body, it is added forever. It is never cut off or cast away.

We may stagger and stumble; we may be unworthy of His grace and love, but we are never ultimately cast aside. When a man is added to the body of Christ, there is something in his heart that is never the same again. He is a new creation in Christ Jesus, and he can never escape it, run away from it, forget it, drown it, or be indifferent to it. To belong to the body of Christ, even though we may be the humblest member, is to be safe in Him. As long as a man's head is above water, you cannot drown his feet. As long as Christ, our head, is in heaven, though I may be but the sole of His feet, I cannot be drowned. I am saved and safe and kept in His forever.

THE DIVINE MYSTERY OF CLEANSING AND SANCTIFICATION

> . . . Christ also loved the church, and gave himself for it;
> That he might sanctify and cleanse it with the washing [*loutron*, meaning "laver," the place where the priests bathed before they entered the house of the Lord] of water by the word (Eph. 5:25–26).

Only one other place in the New Testament is the word *loutron* used.

> Not by works of righteousness which we have done, but according to his mercy he saved us, by the washing [*loutron*] of regeneration, and renewing of the Holy Ghost (Titus 3:5).

Paul uses that word in this passage concerning the church.

The effect of the Word of God is a remarkable thing. When a preacher proclaims it, a church will spring up. As a young man, I did that. I went to a pioneer state in western America, stood in the auditorium of a school house, and preached the gospel for two weeks. We had scores of converts. I baptized them in a stock pond, and immediately they said, "We want to organize a church," and I presided over the organization of the church. When you preach the Word, it bears fruit.

The same preaching of the Word will cleanse and sanctify the church from doctrinal error and keep it right and pure in His sight. Through the preaching of the Word of God, the church is organized according to the Scriptures. It has ordinances and officers according to the Scriptures. Its great doctrinal tenets are according to the Scriptures. When the Word of God is preached, the Spirit of God cleanses the church from all error and doctrinal deviation.

Let me illustrate. I was holding a crusade in a school auditorium in northern Maine. In that part of the world closest to Russia, there is an enormous American Air Force base near Caribou, Maine. When I was there, the head chaplain of that Air Force base was a Northern Baptist. I came to know and love that man of God. One day he said to me, "There is something about you Southern Baptists I do not understand. You do not teach your people doctrines. Just the other day a Southern Baptist couple came to visit me here on the base. They brought their stillborn baby, asking me to baptize the baby because they feared that if I did not, the soul of that baby would be damned to hell forever."

Their fellow airmen, seeing that baby was stillborn, immediately told the father and mother that their child must be baptized or it would spend forever in damnation and hell. Somewhere there was a minister, a Sunday school teacher, an officer in the church who failed to teach pure doctrine to this young couple.

Every child who ever comes into this world is covered, in the atonement of Christ, should he die before he reaches the age of accountability. However, as a child lives his life and reaches the age of accountability, he chooses to do wrong. If he does not confess his sins, repent, and ask God to forgive him of his sins, he is lost. But he is never lost because of the sins of this father or mother or the generations past clear back to Adam. "As in Adam all die even so in Christ shall all be made alive." The atonement of Christ covers that child. When I sin, I am accountable to God, and I must repent and ask God to save me from the judgment upon *my* sins. But that child is saved under the blood, under the atoning grace of the Lord.

The Mystery of Commitment

Husband, love your wives, . . .

For this cause shall a man leave his father and mother, and shall be joined unto his wife, and they two shall be one flesh.

This is a great mystery: but I speak concerning Christ and the church (Eph. 5:25, 31–32).

When you marry, there is a commitment as deep as life itself. When you love your wife and your wife loves you, there is a commitment that is as deep as the soul. Paul says, "This is a great mystery; but I speak concerning Christ and the church." It is unthinkable and unimaginable that there should be a union without commitment. Such would be a contradiction in terms, an anomaly in thought. In the joining of one man and one woman, there is a tremendous commitment, and you will find it in the church that loves Jesus and serves the Lord.

There are many dark places in this earth where all humanity is hopeless, helpless, and sodden. I have seen it all over the earth. Wherever you find such humanity, you will also find there the church, loving and praising the Lord Jesus, pointing the people to hope and help in Him.

In the heart of the Amazon jungle, among crude, stone-age Indians who live a lifetime of murder and spearing one another to death, I have seen the church pointing those violent people to Jesus. We have even had some of them who have been marvelously saved stand in the pulpit of the First Baptist Church of Dallas. Men who have dipped their hands in the blood of missionaries have testified of the Lord Jesus in this pulpit.

I have been in Africa and have seen the lepers who had been cast out into the bush and the jungles to die gathered together by loving hands, ministered unto, treated, and helped. In the midst of the leper colony could be found the church pointing to the love and grace of the blessed Jesus.

I have been under the Arctic Circle preaching in the church the blessed hope of Christ Jesus. Now, you tell me honestly: If you were seeking a man to go to the Arctic Circle or to the depths of the bush and jungle of Africa or to spend his life among stone-age Indians in the Amazon jungle, you would want a man of high courage, great culture, and splendid education. You would ask him to go without earthly reward. Where would you find him? Where would you search for him?

Would you go to Standard Oil Company? Would you go to the great General Motors Corporation? When that General Motors representative goes out, he is going out for stipend. When that representative of Standard Oil goes out, he is going out with a high salary. But, literally, all over this world I have seen gifted, educated, cultured men and women, not expecting earthly reward, travel to the most hostile environment and to the most unacceptable cultures and there give their lives in pointing a sodden humanity to Jesus. That is the church. That is a commitment to Christ that is holy and heavenly.

I am so glad I belong to the family of God, washed in His blood, sanctified in His blood. Lord, Lord, what a good thing You did for me wpen You wrote my name in the Book of Life and placed me, a fellowmember, in the body of Christ.

4

The Well-Ordered Church

Let all things be done decently and in order (1 Cor. 14:40).

If we look at those words "and in order" closely in the Greek text, we find they have far more meaning to us than do the English words "decently" and "order." The Greek word, in its substantive form, is *euschēmonē*. In its adverbial form, the word means "a seeming, becoming manner and way." Many of our English words begin with the prefix "eu," meaning "well," "pleasant," or "beautiful." The word "eucharist" means a beautiful thanksgiving; "eugenics," a splendid inheritance, the genetic foundation of human life; "eulogy," a beautiful word; "euphonic," a beautiful sound; "euphemism," beautiful speaking; "euphoria," beautiful feeling; "euthanasia," beautiful death. In the abridged English dictionary, I counted thirty-eight English words containing that prefix "eu."

The second part of that compound word is schēma, connoting how you respond to the presence of a man, how he impresses you in all of his characteristics, his bearing, grace, speaking, manner, etc.

Paul uses this word to describe our Lord Jesus.

And being found in fashion [*schēma*] as a man, he humbled himself, and became obedient unto death, even the death of the cross (Phil. 2:8).

The word *schēma* refers to all of the impressions that a man gives you through your fives senses. Therefore, the word *eus-*

43

chēmonē refers to a "beautiful presence"—as you see and sense a man or a congregation.

The other word Paul uses is *taxin*, meaning "in order." Josephus uses that word to describe a Roman army camp that was beautifully and felicitously ordered. He uses the same word to describe the worship services of the Essenes, that sect of the Jewish people who lived in the Qumran caves overlooking the Dead Sea and who wrote the Dead Sea Scrolls, one of the greatest archaeological discoveries of all time.

Now Paul uses this word to describe the church. He commends it to us as a congregation of the Lord that is perceived by our five senses as beautifully ordered. In the worship services, in the organization, in the outreach ministries, and in all of the many-faceted programs to which it gives itself, the church ought to be beautifully ordered, behaved, and seen. The impression it gives ought to be godly and heavenly.

THE LOCATION OF A WELL-ORDERED CHURCH

Where would you find such a church? Surely in heaven such a congregation of beautifully behaved saints would be found, but there is no reference here in the Scripture to such a location for that beautifully ordered church of the Lord. When you read the Bible, the beautifully ordered churches were all here on earth. One of them was in Rome; one in Corinth; one in Ephesus; one in Antioch; one in Philippi; one in Thessalonica. They were all located in the teeming cities of the Roman Empire.

For example, the letter of Paul that I have chosen as the background text begins,

> Paul, called to be an apostle of Jesus Christ through the will of God, and Sosthenes our brother,
>
> Unto the church of God which is at Corinth, to them that are sanctified in Christ Jesus, called to be saints, with all that in every place call upon the name of Jesus Christ our Lord, both theirs and ours:
>
> Grace be unto you, and peace, from God our Father, and from the Lord Jesus Christ (1 Cor. 1:1-3).

"The church of God in Corinth"—did you ever see two such diametrical and antithetical opposites brought together in one brief phrase? This congregation loved the Lord, worshiped God, lived in the will and plan of God and had the blessing of God upon it—the church of God in Corinth.

All of those ancient Greek cities were indescribably vile and wicked, licentious in the extreme. But out of all the licentious and iniquitous Greek cities of the ancient world, none was as vile and evil as Corinth. The word "Corinthian" was coined to refer to a debauched and licentious person because the city of Corinth was so evil and depraved. Yet the two are together here—the church of God, i.e., the holy congregation of the Lord, is located in Corinth. Perhaps as the city was more teeming, the presence of the church of the living God was all the more earnestly and deeply and everlastingly needful.

One might easily imagine that God could have programed His people so that the apostle gathered them together to live separated from the world on some beautiful Greek isle. As you know, the Greek archipelago numbers hundreds of such islands.

Lord Byron, the great English poet, makes this exclamation in one of his great poems:

> The isles of Greece, The isles of Greece,
> Where burning Sappho loved and sung.

God did not take His beautiful congregation and separate it from the world. Rather, He placed it in the heart of a teeming city. And the church today seemingly belongs where the thousands and millions of people need the light of heaven to shine upon them.

St. Patrick's Cathedral is in the heart of the isle of Manhattan in New York City. I could not think of London without remembering St. Paul's Cathedral in the very heart of the city with all of those Fleetwood Street newspapers there at the door of that great house of God. I could not think of Paris without calling to mind Notre Dame on that little island in the Seine River in the very center and heart of the capital of France. I could hope that we would not think of the great and growing metropolis of Dallas without remembering the well-ordered, beautiful congregation of God that He has placed in the heart of this city—our own beloved First Baptist Church.

As you know, we have been invited several times to sell our properties. The First Methodist Church has been offered over 20 million dollars for their downtown property, and they have a small portion of land compared to the six blocks our church owns in the heart of Dallas. I do not know how many millions of dollars would be ours if we sold these properties. Think of the beautiful church building we could construct in some section of the city with those millions and millions of dollars. The reason we do not sell lies in the elective purpose and the will of God. He placed those beautiful, well-ordered churches in the heart of the great ancient cities because that is where the church belongs.

One day on the street I met a wonderful man who has an office in one of those tall buildings that looks down upon the city, casting a shadow over our church when the sun rises in the east. He said to me, "I cannot tell you how it affects me when I look out the window of my office and see children on that playground in the heart of this city. It is like nothing I have ever seen in the world." I feel exactly like that fine businessman. How glorious to see children on the church playground, gathered in the name of the Lord. It is a wonderful thing that, amid these skyscrapers and within the teeming life of the insurance, banking, merchandising, wholesaling, and the rest of those businesses and companies that contribute to the intense life of the queenly city of Dallas that in its heart, we also have a lighthouse shining for God.

THE FELLOWSHIP OF A WELL-ORDERED CHURCH

Not only is the location of Corinth as we find it placed by the hands of God in the heart of the city important, but its beautiful fellowship, its caring and compassionate remembrance is also heavenly to behold. The impression you receive when your five senses observe, judge, and describe it is a glorious thing.

For example, in the first pastoral epistle written by Paul to Timothy, his son in the ministry, he says,

> Rebuke not an elder, but entreat him as a father; and the younger men as brethren;
> The elder women as mothers; the younger as sisters, with all purity (5:1–2).

These are marvelous relationships—an older woman is my mother, a younger woman is my sister, an older man is my father, and a younger man is my brother. What a marvelous, beautiful way to see and greet one another and in deference to express love for each other.

In the next verse he speaks of our honoring widows, describing how that beautiful, well-ordered church ought to behave toward the needy, and especially the widow.

We do not realize what the church has done for the world.

The Well-Ordered Church

One time I was in Calcutta, India. In India they have what they call burning vats. Along the banks of the tributary of the Ganges River that flows through Calcutta you can find those burning vats. I stood there several hours and watched that endless procession of Hindus burn their dead. After each body was burned, its remains were thrown into that river. In the river were enormous turtles that lived off the remains of those burned dead. It is to this primitive and pagan place that William Carey, our first great Baptist missionary, went to spend his life. In his day, a widow was burned with the dead body of her husband. Can you imagine the cries of pain and agony when the widow was placed on that burning fire by the side of her dead husband. Even today such a widow is forced to wear certain kinds of clothes and is forbidden to smile. Those things seem barbaric to us, and yet they all have been done in the name of religion. Oh, what a difference the church of the living God has made and does make in the world!

Is there anyone in trouble in our church? Has death entered any home? Is there sorrow or sickness or heartache? In the beautiful, well-ordered church of Christ, the members are there to pray, to encourage, and to lift up. God's well-ordered church is a precious, beautiful thing.

As Paul speaks in this passage about the needy, a verse is striking to me.

> But if any provide not for his own, and specially for those of his own house, he hath denied the faith, and is worse than an infidel (v. 8).

THE FAITH OF A WELL-ORDERED CHURCH

Faith is very much an integral part of the behavior of the child of God. We learn that our Christian faith interacts with every area of our lives—our families, our homes, our businesses, our work, the state, the city, the nation. It is an astonishing discovery if you have not thought it through. We are born into the church one at a time as we are born into this world. We are baptized into the church one at a time by the Holy Spirit of God. It is very personal. But when we are born into the world, when we are born into the kingdom of God, when we are baptized into the fellowship of the church, we are confronted immediately with a plethora of problems, decisions, choices, and interactions.

The letter to the church at Rome is a doctrinal treatise. This letter to the church at Corinth concerns problems that the church faces. There are divisions in the church, and the apostle talks about that. He speaks of incest in the church; then he addresses the matter of litigation in the church; he talks about food offered to idols; then he speaks of marriage and how we are to marry in the Lord; he continues a discussion of how one should dress in the house of God; then he talks about abuses in worship; then he speaks about the ordinances; finally, he comes to the collection for the saints. The Bible reflects our own experiences. We come into the kingdom of God in a great act of faith and commitment, but having come, we are immediately met with decisions and interactions and problems. Many things assailed the church of God in Corinth!

In our world there is a beautiful and wonderful and marvelous strength and encouragement. Paul speaks of it in the encyclical that he wrote to all of the churches, the brief New Testament Book of Ephesians. The first part of Ephesians, chapters 1 through 4, is typical of Paul's letters. It is a discussion of the lofty theme of the heavenlies. Then the last part is a discussion of the problems that we as fathers and mothers and children and workers and masters have in our daily lives. All is a full-orbed revelation of God concerning the church of the Lord in Ephesus. As we face our problems, make our decisions, and live our lives in our modern-day teeming cities and world, the apostle presents to us a challenge for unity and reminds us of the source of strength in our witnessing and living.

> Endeavoring to keep the unity of the Spirit in the bond of peace.
> There is one body, and one Spirit, even as ye are called in one hope of your calling;
> One Lord, one faith, one baptism,
> One God and Father of all, who is above all, and through all, and in you all (Eph. 4:3–6).

What a magnificent benedictory outpouring God has made visible, experiential, and real in the beautifully ordered church—whether in Corinth, in Ephesus, or in Dallas.

He speaks first of the unity of God's holy, informative, guiding Spirit in us all in our work, our homes, and in all to which we pledge heart and hand. When we come together, bringing the Spirit of God in our hearts, think of the beauty and might and power and glory and meaning of our worship in the name of the Lord. We can grieve the Holy Spirit, we can hurt Him, and He can withdraw His blessings from us; but He never leaves us. He is ours forever (John 14:16-17). The Holy Spirit within our hearts guides us, blesses us, strengthens us; and when we come together, we feel the moving of His Spirit within the congregation.

Paul also speaks of the one faith. There is one rule, one order, and one source of instruction and teaching and doctrine for us all—God's inspired, inerrant, infallible Scriptures. Just as there is an objective body of truth for physics or chemistry or astronomy, so there is an objective body of truth in God's rules and regulations for us. As I can hold a book of physics or chemistry or medicine or astronomy in my hand, so I can hold in my hand the objective truth of God's faith—God's written revelation, the Bible. I can read an objective revelation—not esoteric or inward, but outward and objective. One man's idea of God or one man's idea of religion is no better than another man's. God's revelation is not metaphyical. It is not speculative. It is not dubious. It is written down. It is revealed. It is objective. It came from God, not from man. It is to be taught and preached plainly in the congregation of the Lord.

It is like this: one man's idea or speculation concerning the cause and cure of smallpox is not necessarily as good as another man's. When I traveled through the central part of Africa, I came upon a mud house with a thatched roof. In the yard there was an old broom. On the top of the cottage there was another old broom. I did not understand this so I asked about it. The missionary told me that there was smallpox in that house. The cure for smallpox, according to the order of the witch doctor, was to throw an old broom on the top of the roof and another old broom in the yard. I was not surprised when the missionary said that smallpox nearly destroyed that entire tribe that year. The witch doctor's idea about smallpox was not as good as that of Pasteur who discoverd that smallpox is caused by a germ and therefore can be prevented by innoculation and vaccination.

So, with the objective truth of God, one man's speculation or dubious metaphysical searchings or forensics is not as good as what God has said. God has presented and preserved an objective truth that we can read and study for ourselves.

There is one faith, one rule—an objective revelation—and

49

there is one Lord and one God of us all who lives in us, through us, and with us—our wonderful Lord.

People who come to our church are surprised to see a Baptist congregation kneeling to pray. I have our people kneel in the presence of the great God, before whom we are but dust and ashes. It seems appropriate and right to bow and kneel in His presence. In His omnipotent hand He holds the entire creation, and His compassionate love is poured out upon His well-ordered church. It is He who was incarnate in Jesus, our Lord. When I come to Jesus, I come to God. When I love the Lord Jesus, I love God. When I sit at the feet of the Lord Jesus and learn of Him, I learn of God. When I follow the Lord Jesus, I am following God. All of the hearts in the beautiful church are bound together with golden chains that sweep upward from earth to heaven and are held in His dear hands. No man can sever those chains that bind us to the heart of our Lord.

One of the most triumphant chapter endings in all of the Word of God is found in the concluding verses of Romans 8. Paul says,

> For I am persuaded, that neither death, nor life, nor angels, nor principalities, nor powers, nor things present, nor things to come,
> Nor height, nor depth, nor any other creature, shall be able to separate us from the love of God, which is in Christ Jesus our Lord (vv. 38–39).

Oh, Master, what a precious and beautiful open door when You invite us to belong to the family of God!

5

The Ordinances of the Church

> And Jesus came and spake unto them, saying, All power [authority] is given unto me in heaven and in earth.
>
> Go ye therefore, and teach ["disciple," *mathēteusate*—the only imperative in the commission] all nations, baptizing them in the name of the Father, and of the Son, and of the Holy Ghost;
>
> Teaching them to observe all things whatsoever I have commanded you: and, lo, I am with you alway, even unto the end of the world (Matt. 28:18–20).

The Latin word referring to that which is "ordained" or "ordered" is "ordinance." On the basis of the infinite, omnipotent authority of our Lord, He has given us these orders or ordinances. They belong to the church, to the believers who make up the family of God. They do not belong to the congress or to the legislature or to the judiciary or to fraternal organizations or to the city councils. They are preeminently and uniquely placed in the heart of the church.

A Battleground Through the Centuries

These ordinances have been the battleground of forensic confrontation and bitter acrimony from the beginning of the Christian dispensation. Churchmen argue over the number. Are there two or three or five or seven? And they argue over the form and purpose and meaning of those ordinances. They have been used, misused, abused, and endowed with all kinds of esoteric and superstitious overtones.

For example, look at baptism. Its original purpose and

meaning has been changed, and with the change in its meaning came a change in its form. As the years developed there also developed the strange and unusual doctrine that water (like out of a hydrant or creek or pond) could wash away the stain in a man's soul and save him from his sins. As that doctrine was proclaimed and accepted, the question arose, "Then what do you do about your sick?" If the water washes away their sins, then the sick must be subjected to that use of water. Finally, what about the newborn infant? If water washes away sins, then the baby must be placed under the water. With that came a change in the form. Therefore, for the sake of convenience, a few drops of water were sprinkled on the head of the infant or the sick so that their sins were washed away. This is a continuing confrontation in the Christian theological world.

Here is a clipping, a pericope that I took out of *Time* magazine.

> Infant baptism is under fire. The most recent attack on this traditional Christian practice comes from West Germany, where 350 Evangelical (Lutheran) churchmen have petitioned the Rhineland synod to abandon the rubric requiring infant baptism. To give the demand more weight, 50 pastors in Germany have publicly indicated that they will not baptize their own children.
>
> Perhaps the most formidable challenge to infant baptism has been made by Switzerland's venerable Karl Barth, in Part 4 of Volume IV of his masterwork, *Church Dogmatics.* Barth [who was the greatest theologian in this century] argues that there is no biblical basis for infant baptism and that the ritual is not an act of God's grace but a human response to it—which means that the individual must be mature enough to understand the meaning of such a decision. The traditional understanding of the sacrament, he says, is simply "an old error of the church."
>
> St. Augustine articulated the gloomy theology of baptism that was to remain current in the Church for nearly 1,000 years [until the reformation] that the ritual was necessary to cleanse an individual of the stain of original sin, and that the unbaptized were doomed to hell. Somewhat more merciful in his thinking Thomas Aquinas later suggested that the unbaptized would go not to hell but to limbo, though original sin would still deny them heaven.
>
> A growing number of Roman Catholic thinkers now look on original sin as the universal weakness of a man rather than a damning individual fault—which cuts the ground out completely from the need for infant baptism. Still others object to the "magical" implications of the baptism ceremony—namely, that a spiritual cleansing is achieved by the physical act of pouring a few drops of water on the infant's head.

There is no doubt but that through the years and the centuries and even today, the ordinances are a battleground for theological confrontation.

The Lord's Supper is no different. It also is a bone of bitter contention. Even a schoolboy knows that when the great reformers sought to present a united front in the Reformation of the church, they vigorously and hopelessly divided themselves over the meaning of the Lord's Supper. One of the famous confrontations was between Martin Luther and Zwingli, and finally they separated—never to agree.

When I went to the seminary, one of my learned professors taught that a person should not take the Lord's Supper except in the church to which he belonged. As I listened to this learned ecclesiastic, I thought, "How strange." Paul observed the Lord's Super with the Christians in Troas; yet he did not belong to that church. He spoke of the memorial supper at great length as he taught the people in Corinth, even though he did not belong to the church in Corinth. You can go to any theological library and find volumes and volumes discussing those altercations and confrontations over the ordinances of the church.

THE PLAIN, SIMPLE PURPOSE OF CHRIST

First, to me the ordinances are nothing but the plain and simple effort on the part of the Lord Jesus to place in dramatic form and human experience the great fundamental truths of the gospel.

> And this gospel of the kingdom shall be preached in all the world for a witness unto all nations; and then shall the end come (Matt. 24:14).

That means that if the gospel of Christ is preached through all the nations of the world, it has to be translated into different tongues and dialects, and it has to be presented to people of strange cultures and customs. Not only that, but many times the gospel is translated and presented to strange tribes and families and people by men who themselves are uneducated, untrained, unequipped. Under such conditions, how do you keep pure the great fundamental truths of the faith?

Christ, in His infinite wisdom took the common experience of all men everywhere and placed in those common human

experiences the tremendously meaningful, foundational, fundamental truths of the gospel. All men everywhere eat and drink.
All men everywhere know death and burial. The Lord took those
common universal human experiences and sealed in them the
great truths of the gospel. The bread that we break is His body.
The crushed fruit of the vine that we drink is the crimson of His
life. That protrays His atoning suffering. In Romans, Paul
eloquently describes the burial in water.

> Know ye not, that so many of us as were baptized into Jesus
> Christ were baptized unto his death?
> Therefore we are buried with him by baptism into death: that
> like as Christ was raised up from the dead by the glory of the Father,
> even so we also should walk in newness of life (6:3–4).

In 1 Corinthians Paul defines the gospel.

> Moreover, brethren, I declare unto you the gospel which I
> preached unto you, which also ye have received, and wherein ye
> stand;
> By which also ye are saved, if ye keep in memory what I
> preached unto you, unless ye have believed in vain.
> For I delivered unto you first of all that which I also received,
> how that Christ died for our sins according to the scriptures;
> And that he was buried, and that he rose again the third day
> according to the scriptures (15:1–4).

Those common experiences of universal life and death now
bear the burden of the truth of the gospel. Eating the bread and
drinking the fruit of the vine are pictures of His atoning grace,
and being buried and raised to life portrays to the world the marvelous promise of God to us who have found refuge in Him.

THE ORDINANCES PREACH THE GOSPEL TO THE EYE

The ordinance that the Lord has instituted is a dramatic presentation of the gospel to the eye as the preaching of the Word is
the presentation of the gospel to the ear. We witness to the truth
of the grace of God in our preaching.

> For after that in the wisdom of God the world by wisdom knew
> not God, it pleased God by the foolishness of preaching to save
> them that believe (1 Cor. 1:21).

We not only witness to the ear but we witness to the eye as well,
both by the water and by the bread and the crushed fruit of the

vine. These are dramatic presentations of the great message of the grace of God in Christ Jesus.

For example, our Lord will say

> . . . Take, eat: this is my body, which is broken for you: this do in remembrance of me.
>
> After the same manner also he took the cup, when he had supped, saying, This cup is the new testament in my blood; this do ye, as oft as ye drink it, in remembrance of me.
>
> For as often as ye eat this bread, and drink this cup, ye do show [portray, dramatize, proclaim] the Lord's death till he come (1 Cor. 11:24–26).

The ordinances are a dramatization to the human eye of the great truth of the gospel. They do not procure our salvation; they proclaim it. They do not possess magic; they bear witness to a majestic truth. They do not expiate our sins; they exhibit the atoning love and grace of our Lord. They proclaim the gospel message.

They are memorials. We could never forget these tremendous monuments to what Christ has done for us. They are visible. They are effective. They are glorious.

Near Boston is the Bunker Hill Monument. It reminds us of the men who fought in the Revolutionary War for our colonies' independence. In the heart of the capital city of America stands the great Washington Monument to help us remember the dedication of that general who was the father of our country. Hodgenville, Kentucky, has one of the most effective monuments in the world—a beautiful marble edifice built over a humble log cabin. On the portico facing the south these words are engraved: "With malice toward none, with charity for all." That is the place where Abraham Lincoln was born. Near Houston stands the tall San Jacinto Monument that reminds us of Sam Houston and his little group of straggling soldiers who won independence for Texas.

In the same way these ordinances are memorials. They are monuments enduring forever, recalling to our hearts what Christ has done for us and promised to us. These other monuments crumble with the passing of time, but the ordinances—these memorials of our Savior—are recreated again and again in every human experience. They are beautiful to behold and thrice wonderful when we know what they mean and what they proclaim.

They Were Never Meant to Save the Souls of Men

It was never the thought of our Lord, nor is it ever suggested in the Holy Scriptures that these ordinances will procure our salvation or that they are means of grace by which we are saved. If rite and ritual and ceremony and ordinance could have saved us, there would never have been any need for our Savior to come into the world to suffer and to die for our sins.

In your Bible, you will find not just verses, not just paragraphs, not just chapters, but you will find books in the Old Testament filled with the rites and ceremonies and ordinances presided over by officiating, mediating priests. If those rites and rituals and ceremonies and ordinances could have saved us, Jesus would never have had to come.

The whole Book of Hebrews concerns that great truth, especially the heart of the book, chapters 9 and 10. The marvelous preacher who wrote the Book of Hebrews is saying to us that the blood of bulls and goats and the ordinances and ceremonies presided over by officiating priests could never make us perfect before God, nor could they ever make atonement for our sins.

If we could wash our own sins away, we would do it. Why would we need a Savior to come and die for us? If another man could wash our sins away, we would not need our dear Savior to come and die for us. If there was anything we could do to save ourselves, we would not need a Savior.

The ordinances, the rituals, the ceremonies only point us to Him who has made it possible for us to be forgiven of our sins through His grace, love, suffering, and atoning death. We sing that all the time.

> What can wash away my sin?
> Nothing but the blood of Jesus;
> What can make me whole again?
> Nothing but the blood of Jesus.
>
> O! precious is the flow
> That makes me white as snow;
> No other fount I know,
> Nothing but the blood of Jesus.

This is the gospel. It is never found in ritual or ceremony or ordinance or mediating priests. It is always one of the atoning grace and love of our Lord. This is the way I am saved according to the Word of God. I am not saved by my own works but by God's grace.

> For by grace are ye saved through faith; and that not of yourselves: it is the gift of God:
> Not of works, lest any man should boast (Eph. 2:8–9).

When you get to heaven, you will not lift up your voice and your hands in praise saying, "All glory to me. Look what I did! I did it!" When you get to heaven and you lift up your voice to sing with the hosts of glory, you will proclaim "Worthy is the Lamb that was slain, who has redeemed us by His blood out of every tribe and family and people and race and tongue!" It is all glory to Him. We will not enter heaven by our merit but by His merit.

> Not by works of righteousness which we have done, but according to his mercy he saves us, by the washing of regeneration, and renewing of the Holy Ghost (Titus 3:5).

How beautifully simple God has made that way into heaven! Even a child can understand it. I accepted Christ when I was ten years old. I know a man who said to me, "I was wonderfully saved when I was six years old."

The way of our Lord is always a plain and simple way and especially so when God tells us how to be saved. If He made it difficult and recondite and hard to understand, we might have missed it. But He makes it plain and simple, and the ordinances so present it. We are saved by turning from our own way. The Bible describes that with the Greek word *metanoia,* which is translated "repentance" or "turning." If I am out in the world following my own selfish goals and visions and aims, God asks me to turn and look to Jesus. That is biblical repentance. By turning and accepting I am saved. I open my heart heavenward and Christward and Godward. The Lord comes into my heart, my home, my life, and my work. That is acceptance. God comes into my heart and sanctifies every dream and prayer of my soul. He writes my name in the Book of Life, and He stands by me as a fellow pilgrim. And in the hours of death He will send an angel to take me to heaven. God has done a wonderful thing. Those wonderful, foundational, fundamental saving truths are these that are presented in that humble beautiful ordinance—to break bread, to drink the cup, to be buried and raised in baptism.

In my study and preparation I read of a martyr in the second Christian century. He was a nobleman who was called before the king. The king said to him in anger, "You renounce that Christian faith and recant the giving of your life to Christ. If you do not, I will banish you from the kingdom!" His nobleman replied, "Oh, king, I belong to the kingdom of Christ and He said, 'I will never leave thee nor forsake thee.'" The infuriated king said, "I will not only banish you if you do not recant the faith and disown and reject this Christ, I will confiscate everything you possess!" The nobleman replied, "Oh, king, my possessions are in heaven. My treasures are above, and they cannot be touched." The king exclaimed, "I will slay you before my very eyes! I will execute you here if you do not renounce that faith!" The nobleman replied, "Sir, these many years I have been dead with Christ and buried with Him, and my life is hid with Christ in God."

How do you abolish or banish a cadaver? How do you slay a corpse? When a man is dead with Christ and buried with our Lord, you cannot insult him; he is dead. You cannot hurt him; he is dead. You cannot take away from him; he is dead.

I would to God that I could fully comprehend that state of being dead with Christ. I cannot be insulted. I cannot be hurt. I cannot be grieved. I am dead with the Lord. My life is hid with Christ in God. I am alive to Him. Oh, Lord, that I could be sensitive to God's will and God's cause and follow the pilgrim way that leads from earth to heaven.

That is the meaning of the ordinance. We remember in a memorial His sacrifice for us—breaking bread and drinking the cup. And we are buried with Him—dead to the world—and we are raised with Him. We have a new life and a new hope with God.

6

The Divine Institution of Baptism

In the heart of the Great Commission, you will find that our Savior commanded this strange and unusual rite.

> And Jesus came and spake unto them, saying, All power [authority] is given unto me in heaven and in earth.
>
> Go ye therefore, and teach [*mathēteuō*, meaning "make disciples"] all nations, baptizing them in the name of the Father, and of the Son, and of the Holy Spirit.
>
> Teaching them to observe all things whatsoever I have commanded you: and, lo, I am with you alway, even unto the end of the world (Matt. 28:18–20).

As our Savior looked down through the corridor of the years that lay before Him, He saw in every age and generation thousands upon thousands who would be standing in pools, ponds, creeks, rivers, oceansides, and baptistries. He saw thousands of others looking upon that unusual ordinance. Down through the ages there have been great out pourings of the Spirit of God followed by the great baptismal services that completed their union to our Lord in a unique way.

For example, in Acts 2 we are told of 3,000 who were baptized at Pentecost. In Acts 19, we are told that all Asia turned to the Lord and that they were baptized into the communion and faith of the Lord Jesus. In A.D. 404, John Chrysostom, the golden-mouthed preacher, baptized 3,000 soldiers on Easter in Constantinople, the capital of the Roman Empire. In A.D. 430, Patrick of Ireland baptized the king, his son, and 12,000 men. Clovis, King of France was baptized, together with 3,000 soldiers from his army, in A.D. 496. In A.D. 597, in Canterbury, Augustine, the missionary to the Anglo-Saxons of England, baptized 10,000 men, with each man baptizing the other one, and then "an infinite number of women and children," according to the history book. From A.D. 680 to 755, Boniface, a martyred saint who was an English missionary to the Teutonic tribes of Germany, often baptized many thousands at once and over 100,000 in his lifetime. Between A.D. 980 and 1015, Vladimir of Kiev, the first Tzar of Russia, who himself was converted to the Christian faith, led hundreds of thousands of his subjects through the baptismal waters. Our great Anabaptist forefather Balthasar Hubmaier, who was burned at the stake in Vienna, March 10, 1528, baptized from 6,000 to 12,000 converts every year. In India, in 1878, six missionaries baptized 2,222 Telugus in one day.

The last time I visited South Korea, I was asked to remain for the Lord's Day. The church there wanted me to speak to 1,400 South Korean soldiers who were going to be baptized. I had to begin a crusade in Hong Kong on Sunday and could not stay. I wish I could have seen that marvelous living testimony to our Lord's death, burial, and resurrection.

In presiding over a meeting of the Baptist World Alliance, I heard two Burmese pastors speak of the thousands and thousands who are being baptized today in that communist-dominated land. Our Lord saw those uncounted numbers in their generations coming into the faith and then to the baptismal waters. It is meaningful to us who walk through the waters of baptism and no less to those who look upon the ordinance.

Therefore, as I look upon baptism—that holy and initial ordinance, I think of it in three great categories:(1) its historical truth, (2) its experiential truth, and (3) its prophetic truth—i.e., its revealed past, its meaningful present , and its unfolding future.

ITS HISTORICAL TRUTH

For four hundred years there was silence from heaven. No prophet appeared to the people of God. Then came the startling appearance of John the Baptist and the strange rite he administered in the Jordan River. Our Lord Jesus walked the sixty miles from Nazareth in Galilee down to the Jordan to be baptized of John. The first step of our Lord in His public messianic ministry was to be baptized by the great prophet, John the Baptist.

At the baptism of Christ, we see for the first time in recorded history all three persons of the Godhead actively presented. The voice of the Father came from heaven, "This is my beloved Son, in whom I am well pleased." The Holy Spirit descended bodily in the form of a dove. The Son of God submitted Himself to the rite.

Our Savior here pledged Himself for the redemption of our souls from sin. In keeping with the prophetic promise in Daniel 9, it is thus that our Savior gave Himself to make an end to sin and to bring in everlasting righteousness. He said to John, ". . . for thus it becometh us to fulfill all righteousness" (Matt. 3:15). In that holy ordinance the Lord pledged Himself to die for us that we might be washed from our sins and raised from among the dead for our justification. In that tremendous beginning we have the introduction of the dispensation of the age of grace. I know that because in Acts, the qualification of an apostle is that he had to be baptized by John the Baptist. This is the introduction of a new *oikonomia,* a new dispensation, a new age of grace, the age of preaching of the saving gospel of the Son of God. Thus its historical past is full of deep, revealed meaning for us.

ITS EXPERIENTIAL TRUTH

By the experiential present, I mean the unfolding of the meaning of baptism in our own lives. The ordinance of baptism is something that we share in our hearts when we listen to the gospel message of Christ. It is our first response in faith to the Lord. We have the same experience that the treasurer of Ethiopia had when he listened to Philip the evangelist as described in Acts 8. He was reading in Isaiah and came to 53:6, "All we like sheep have gone astray; we have turned every one to his own way; and the LORD hath laid on him the iniquity of us all." As the Ethiopian treasurer read, he turned to the evangelist Philip and said,

> . . . of whom speaketh the prophet this? of himself, or of some other man?
>
> Then Philip opened his mouth, and began at the same scripture, and preached unto him Jesus.
>
> And as they went on their way, they came unto a certain water: and the eunuch said, See, here is water; what doth hinder me to be baptized?
>
> And Philip said, If thou believest with all thine heart, thou mayest. And he answered and said, I believe that Jesus Christ is the Son of God.

> And he commanded the chariot to stand still: and they went down both into the water, both Philip and the eunuch; and he baptized him.
>
> And when they were come up out of the water, the Spirit of the Lord caught away Philip, that the eunuch saw him no more: and he went on his way rejoicing (Acts 8:34–39).

This should be our response to the gospel. When I have accepted Jesus as my Savior, my first reply ought to be "I want to be baptized."

It is in baptism that we are made one with Him. Notice that little pronoun "us" in the words our Lord said to John the Baptist: "Thus it becometh *us* to fulfill all righteousness"; He includes us with Him, and He submits Himself to an ordinance that we are to share alike. "Thus it becometh *us*." We are united with our Lord in that holy ordinance.

It is a remarkable thing how the apostle Paul writes of that ordinance.

> Moreover, brethren, I would not that ye should be ignorant, how that all our fathers were under the cloud, and all passed through the sea;
>
> And were all baptized unto Moses in the cloud and in the sea (1 Cor. 10:1–2).

The Israelites were joined with their great lawgiver and deliverer and leader. They were united with him in the baptism of the cloud and in the baptism of the sea. In the midst of the shekinah glory of God and in the midst of their deliverance from the waters of the Red Sea, Moses and his people were one.

Thus it is in our holy ordinance of baptism. We are joined to Christ. We are united with Him. We are one with Him—in His death, in His burial, and in His resurrection. It is an experience of our lives, our souls, our hearts. We feel it; we respond to it, and God says, "I am well pleased."

During the time I was a college student at Baylor, between Fourth Street and the Brazos River, there was a large slum area filled with poor and ragged people. Every afternoon I would take my Bible and go down into that area of the city of Waco. Going from house to house, knocking from door to door, I introduced myself to those who opened the door, "I am a young minister in school and I want to know if you are Christians here?" If they said Yes, then I would ask to come in and read the Bible with them and pray. If they told me they were not Christians, then I would ask if I could come in and show them how to be saved.

One afternoon, as I returned to the campus, I was walking through the famous Oak Grove Cemetery. I met a man in the cemetery who was just finishing up his work for the day and was about ready to go home. I began to talk to him. He was not a Christian; in fact, he was an infidel. I expressed my amazement that in this great circle of the tokens of our mortality and the brevity of life, he should not believe. As I pleaded with him and spoke to him, we knelt in prayer, one on each side of a grave. I poured out my heart to God for him. As I prayed for him, I extended my hand to him across the grave and asked him if at that moment he would receive Christ as his personal Savior. He warmly grasped my hand and replied, "I will." Then I thanked God for him, and we stood up. He went on his way to make a confession in the church and to follow the Lord in baptism.

In one of those strange coincidences that I could never explain, the grave that we knelt beside was that of Dr. B. H. Carroll, the head of the Bible Department at Baylor and the founder of Southwestern Baptist Theological Seminary. He also had been an unbeliever—a blatant one, a forensic and argumentative one. He was wounded and crippled while serving in the Confederate Army during the Civil War, and he came out a bitter infidel, blaspheming the name of God. Then he was marvelously, wonderfully converted. I have never read a sermon that was more meaningful or moving than B. H. Carroll's sermon entitled, "My Infidelity and What Became of It." He describes how he turned from unbelief to faith, from the world to God, from darkness to light, and then he describes his baptism.

> I will never forget the day I was baptized. Oh, dear friends, if you could ever know, God grant that you may never know esperientially, the horrors of hell through which I passed in my infidelity. But when the Lord God converted my soul and I saw my dear Redeemer, when I gave myself to Him without reserving one atom, I said, "Lord Jesus, write thy name on my head and let it think for thee, on my hands and let them work for thee, and on my feet and let them walk for thee; write it, Lord, all over me, for I am altogether thine."
>
> Then, lovingly, I said, "Lord what do you want me to do? I am going to do it. I will do what my Master commands me to do." And when I took His Book and read about baptism, I came up to the

church and I said, "I want you to hear a statement that I have to make. I have been converted." And that cold day I stood up and told the story. There was a bitter norther blowing, but my heart was warm.

I just gave them the whole story: "Now, brethren, I do, trustfully and lovingly receive the Lord Jesus Christ as my Savior, and I want to be baptized." And I went down to the creek, and that dear pupil of Dr. Burleson's, the President of Baylor, who was called the Spurgeon of Texas, W. W. Harris [He was the first pastor of this church, and we have named one of our buildings the Spurgeon-Harris Building] led me down into the water, in old David's Creek in Burleson County. I see that creek today in my mind, and when my feet walked down into the water, I thought of my burial; that the time would come when I would be dead; when my body would be cold; when it would be put out of sight [the grave over which I led that man to the Lord]; and in advance of death, I was erecting a monument that would tell death, that it should not hold me forever, and my heart was glad. Then followed my burial with Christ and my rising with Christ. And when I came up out of the water, and the old brethren gathered around me. Oh, the joy of it, the glory of it, following Jesus.

It is an experiential truth—all of me baptized, not just a part. As Paul writes,

> I beseech you therefore, brethren, by the mercies of God, that ye present your bodies a living sacrifice, holy, acceptable unto God, which is your reasonable service (Rom. 12:1).

Did you notice what Dr. Carroll said? "I give you my head to think for thee; I give you my hands to work for thee; I give you my feet to walk for thee." All of me is to be devoted to the Lord. All of me is to be baptized, joined to Christ, united to Him.

Something funny happened once in our baptistry at the First Baptist Church. A man was coming down for me to baptize him. When he got almost into the water, he stopped and said, "Oh, wait a minute, pastor, I forgot to take out my billfold." I said, "That's all right, brother, come on in. All my life I have wanted to baptize a man's billfold!" All of me is joined to the dear Lord.

Paul has a magnificent word to say about that:

> For as many of you as have been baptized into Christ have put on Christ (Gal. 3:27).

It is like a man who is in an army. He puts on the uniform of his country, and he marches under the flag and in the name of the nation that is the home of his family and the center of the devotion of his patriotic allegiance. Thus it is with us. As many of us as have been baptized into Jesus Christ have put on Christ. We are clothing ourselves with our blessed Lord. It is an experiential truth. It is something in our souls, lives, hearts, devotion, and commitment.

ITS PROPHETIC TRUTH

It is the commitment to a belief in a great miracle in the unfolding future. That miracle is the physical resurrection of our bodies.

It is an unusual thing when you read from these men who are so scholarly and learned. Many of them say that the highwater mark of all biblical revelation is found in 1 Corinthians 15. That is the great resurrection chapter of the Bible. Paul writes,

> Moreover, brethren, I declare unto you the gospel which I preached unto you, which also ye have received, and wherein ye stand;
> By which also ye are saved, if ye keep in memory what I preached unto you, unless ye have believed in vain.
> For I delivered unto you first of all that which I also received, how that Christ died for our sins according to the scriptures;
> And that he was buried, and that he rose again the third day according to the scriptures. (vv. 1–4).

When a man preaches the gospel, he preaches that Jesus died for our sins, He was buried, and He was raised for our justification.

The rest of 1 Corinthians 15 is a presentation of our physical resurrection from among the dead. That is an astonishing revelation. I cannot hide from it; I stagger before it many times. I live in a world of death and burial, of weeping and heartache, of separation and sorrow. If there is a death, a pastor is almost the first one told. I share in many of those memorial services. I see babies lowered into the ground still and silent.

That these shall live again and be raised from the dust of the ground is the heart of the gospel. What gives vitality and viability and power and strength and glory to the preaching of the gospel is that on the third day Christ was raised from the dead and ascended into heaven. He is not our dead Lord but our living Lord, and some day He is coming again. Because He lives, we shall live also; and if we are buried with Him, we shall also be raised with Him. That is a doctrine unique to the Christian faith. It is found nowhere else in the earth.

All of the ancients believed in the immortality of the soul. The Book of the Dead, the hieroglyphics that surround those who are buried in Egypt, tells about the life beyond. All of the ancient Greeks believed that beyond that dark River Styx there was some kind of a shadowy immortality. Even the American Indian was buried with his bow and arrow because he believed that he would need it in the Happy Hunting Ground.

But when Paul preached the resurrection of the physical body before the Areopagus, the Supreme Court in Athens, the Epicureans scoffed and laughed aloud. They were atomic atheists. They taught that the world was made of atoms. That sounds very modern, does it not? They taught that the coarser atoms made up the human body and then went back to the dust and that the finer atoms were the soul and were diffused into the world. When they heard of the ressurection of the dead, they guffawed and laughed in scorn.

The Stoics were more genteel. They were pantheists. They believed that everything was a part of a world soul and that when we died we went back and were dissolved into that world soul. But the resurrection of our physical body was unthinkable to the Stoic philospher, and he just quietly smiled and bowed away.

Lord, is it possible that these hands that decay in death will be recreated and immortalized and that they will serve Thee? These eyes that fall into disintegration and decay, will be resurrected and immortalized and see Thee? Could it be?

I think of the great avowal of Job:

> For I know that my Redeemer liveth, and that he shall stand at the latter day upon the earth:
> And though after my skin worms destroy this body, yet in my flesh shall I see God:
> Whom I shall see for myself, and mine eyes shall behold, and not another . . . (Job 19:25–27a).

Lord, give me greater faith, give me greater commitment, give me greater consecration. What a blessedness! What a preciousness! That grave is not the end. That corruption is not final. That darkness that lies beyond this life is not forever midnight despair. Beyond the grave is resurrection; beyond death there is life; beyond the darkness there is light and immortality. It is the gift of God in the resurrection of His dear Son. That faith and that hope is expressed in my baptism. I am baptized, buried in the likeness of His death, and I am raised in the glorious hope of *His* and *my* resurrection.

7

The Baptism God Commands

> And Jesus came and spake unto them, saying, All power [authority] is given unto me in heaven and in earth.
>
> Go ye therefore [on the basis of that authoritarian, sovereign majesty of our Master] and teach [*mathēteusate,* an imperative command meaning "to make disciples"] all nations, baptizing them in the name of the Father, and of the Son, and of the Holy Ghost:
>
> Teaching them to observe all things whatsoever I have commanded you: and, lo, I am with you alway, even unto the end of the world. Amen (Matt. 28:18–20).

In the heart of that Great Commission there is a mandate for the disciples who are won to Christ to be baptized. Baptism is the first church ordinance we are commanded to keep.

SETTING THE STAGE FOR THE NEW COVENANT

As I study the Bible, it is apparent that this new age of grace began with a commanded holy ordinance. A Greek New Testament is embossed with the Greek words *Kainos Diathēkē,* which means "The New Commandment." The new covenant began with a baptizing preacher.

> In those days came John the Baptist, preaching in the wilderness of Judea. . . .
>
> Then went out to him Jerusalem, and all Judea, and all the region round about Jordan,
>
> And were baptized of him in Jordan, confessing their sins (Matt. 3:1, 5–6).

The gospel of Mark begins,

The Baptism God Commands

The beginning of the gospel of Jesus Christ, the Son of God.

John did baptize in the wilderness, and preach the baptism of repentance for the remission of sins.

And there went out unto him all the land of Judea, and they of Jerusalem, and were all baptized of him in the river of Jordan, confessing their sins (Mark 1:1, 4–5).

The sainted apostle John began that new dispensation like this:

In the beginning was the Word, and the Word was with God, and the Word was God.

There was a man sent from God, whose name was John.

And they asked him, and said unto him, Why baptizest thou then, if thou be not that Christ, nor Elijah, neither that prophet? (John 1:1, 6, 25).

Thus this new era of grace started with a baptizing preacher, to whom God gave the name "John." In Greek, *Yōannēs,* and in Hebrew, *Yohanan,* means "God is gracious." The angel Gabriel appeared unto the priest Zechariah.

But the angel said unto him, Fear not, Zechariah: for thy prayer is heard; and thy wife Elisabeth shall bear thee a son, and thou shalt call his name John.

And Zechariah said unto the angel, Whereby shall I know this? for I am an old man, and my wife well stricken in years.

And the angel answering said unto him, I am Gabriel, that stand in the presence of God; and am sent to speak unto thee, and to show thee these glad tidings.

And, behold, thou shalt be dumb, and not able to speak, until the day that these things shall be performed, because thou believest not my words, which shall be fulfilled in their season.

Now Elisabeth's full time came that she should be delivered; and she brought forth a son.

And it came to pass, that on the eighth day they came to circumcise the child; and they called him Zechariah, after the name of his father.

And his mother answered and said, Not so; but he shall be called John.

And they said unto her, There is none of thy kindred that is called by this name.

And they made signs to his father, how he would have him called.

And he asked for a writing table, and wrote, saying, His name is John. And they marveled all.

And his mouth was opened immediately, and his tongue loosed, and he spake, and praised God (Luke 1:13, 18–20, 57, 59–64).

69

A man was sent from God, and God said his name was John. The Holy Scriptures called him *Yōannēs ho Baptistēs,* John the Baptist.

In the New Testament, the word "Christian" is used three times, and the word "Baptist" fourteen times. According to the word of God, John was the first great preacher of the kingdom of our Lord. He belongs to the new dispensation, this age of grace.

For example, our Savior says,

> The law and the prophets were until [one Greek text will have *heos;* another will have *mechri.* Both are adverbs of time and mean "as far as" or "until" or "extended to"] John: since that time the kingdom of God is preached, and every man presseth into it (Luke 16:16).

We cannot enter the exciting, startling, sudden, Elijah-like appearance of this wilderness "baptizing" preacher. All Jerusalem emptied out as the people went to hear him. People from the towns in Judea and Perea on the other side of the Jordan River and all of the area surrounding the Jordan came by the thousands to the river to listen to John the Baptist announce the coming kingdom. I just cannot imagine the electrifying effect of such an announcement as that.

For example, our Lord speaks of John: "But what went ye out for to see? . . ." He repeats the question in the next verse, "But what went ye out for to see? . . ." (Matt. 18:8a, 9a). The inhabitants of the entire countryside as well as people from the cities had gone to see and to hear this prophet sent from heaven to announce the new dispensation.

According to the first chapter of the Gospel of John, among the thousands who were there to question him was an officially appointed committee of the Sanhedrin.

> And this is the record of John, when the Jews sent priests and Levites from Jerusalem to ask him, Who art thou?
>
> And he confessed, and denied not; but confessed, I am not the Christ.
>
> And they asked him, What then? Art thou Elijah? And he saith, I am not. Art thou that prophet? And he answered, No.
>
> Then said they unto him. Who art thou? that we may give an answer to them that sent us. What sayest thou of thyself?
>
> He said, I am THE VOICE OF ONE CRYING IN THE WILDERNESS, MAKE STRAIGHT THE WAY OF THE LORD, as said the prophet Isaiah (John 1:19–23).

The Baptism God Commands

Every preacher ought to be like John. The true preacher does not invent his message. He is an ambassador from the courts of heaven, and he delivers only what God says. A genuine preacher is a voice, an echo; he repeats what God has written in the Bible. John was a voice from God crying in the wilderness, "Make ready the way of the Lord."

Then the religious leaders asked him, "Where did you get this ordinance? If you are not the Christ, if you are not Elijah, if you are not a prophet, where did you get your authority?"

John replied, "I got it from heaven. God sent me to baptize." This is the initial ordinance of the kingdom of our Lord. Baptism began as the symbol of the resurrection power, recreating the ableness of Jesus our Lord.

In the Bible there is a Greek word that is not translated. It is the Greek word *baptizō*. Because the translators belonged to the Anglican church, they took this very special, precise word to the king and said, "What shall we do with this word?" The translators and the king agreed that they would Anglicize rather than translate the word. Thus, the Greek word *baptizō* became "baptize."

What does the word mean? What was John doing in the Jordan River when the Scripture says he was "baptizing"? *Baptizō* is a common Greek word, the meaning of which has not changed in thousands of years. I am going to let you determine an accurate translation by seeing its usage by the great Greek historians, geographers, philosophers, and professional men.

Hippocrates lived from 460 to 377 B.C. He was the "Father of Medicine." Describing the respiration of a patient affected with inflammation and swelling of the throat, he wrote:

> As she breathed, she breathed as a person breathes after having been *baptizō*.

The great philosopher Aristotle lived 384–322 B.C., and said:

> The Phoenicians sailing beyond Hercules Pillars [beyond Gibraltar] came to a land uninhabited, whose coast was full of seaweeds, and is not laid under water at ebb, but when the tide comes in, it is wholly *baptizō*.

Here is a sentence from Heraclides who flourished about 325 B.C. He wrote the "Homeric Allegories." He was a disciple of Aristotle, and while moralizing on the fable of Mars being taken by Vulcan, he says:

> Neptune is ingeniously supposed to deliver Mars from Vulcan to signify that when a piece of iron is taken red-hot out of a fire, and *baptizo* into water, the heat is repelled and extinguished.

Polybius lived 204–122 B.C. A great historian, he describes a spear:

> Even if the spear falls into the sea it is not lost, for it is compacted of oak and pine so that when the heavy part is *baptizō* by the weight, the rest is buoyed up and it is easily recovered.

That is, the head of the spear sinks into the water, but the handle of the spear floats on top of the water so that you can easily recover it.

Polybius, describing in his history the passage of soldiers through the river Febia, which had been swollen during the night by heavy rains like the ones we have along the Ohio and the Wabash, says,

> They crossed with difficulty, those on foot *baptizō* as far as the breast.

Diodorus, a Roman historian who lived in 60 B.C., wrote these words:

> The river rushing down with the current, increased in violence and *baptizō* many.
>
> Most of the wild animals surrounded by the stream perished, being *baptizō* but some escaping to the high grounds, were saved.

Strabo, a contemporary of our Savior, was a historian and a geographer. Writing in Greek, he said,

> One who hurls down a dart from above into the channel, the force of the water makes so much resistance that it is hardly *baptizō*.

Strabo, in his geography, was describing the mark of Alexander's soldiers on the occasion when they were passing between the mountain Climax and the Pamphilian Sea, a land often subject to overflow during heavy storms. Strabo says:

> It happened that the whole day long the march was made in water, the men being *baptizō* up to the waist.

Flavius Josephus was an illustrious and famous Jewish historian who lived in the time of the apostles—Paul, John, and Peter. He wrote his histories in Greek. From Josephus we read his description of the murder of a ruler,

> And stretching out the right hand so as to be unseen by any, he
> *baptizō* the whole sword into his body.

Here is still another instance from the Greek poet Julian.
Those Greek poets had the most beautiful way of saying things.
Julian describes love as a tickling on the inside, something that is
all over the inside of you:

> As I once trimmed a garland
> I found Cupid in the roses.
> Holding him by the wings,
> I *baptizō* him into wine,
> And took him and drank him
> And now within my members,
> He tickles with his wings.

Could you think of a more beautiful way to describe falling in
love than what the poet describes as "That tickling with Cupid's
wings"?

Notice the word *baptizō*. It is an ordinary Greek word,
meaning "immerse, dip." There is no exception to that in the
thousands of years of Greek literature. The word is used again
and again, but I have chosen only a few examples. It cannot be
translated any other way.

What was John doing in the Jordan River? He was burying
those people in the water and raising them up to a new life in the
kingdom of our Lord.

The Jews had many ablutions. They washed their pots and
pans; they washed their feet and hands; they bathed themselves
all over. But in the Old Testament, in the apocrypha, in Philo, in
Josephus, the devotee always washed or cleansed himself. But
this was new and different—John took another and washed him
(baptized him) in administering this ordinance in the Jordan
River. That is why the committee from Jerusalem said, "Where
did you get this new ordinance? By what authority do you intro-
duce this new rite?" John replied, "I got it from God."

BEGINNING A NEW LIFE IN CHRIST

We are introduced into the kingdom of our Savior with the
symbolic rite of baptism. The new life in Christ begins with this
initial ordinance.

> John did baptize in the wilderness, and preach the baptism of
> repentance for the remission of sins (Mark 1:4).

73

John preached that the ordinance of baptism is a sign and symbol of repentance *(metanoia,* describing a man's decision to turn when he gives his heart to Christ). Baptism is not the change itself; rather, it is a sign or symbol of that turning. When a man wears a wedding ring, the ring is not a marriage; it is a sign of marriage. When the flag is raised, the flag is not the nation; it is the symbol of that nation. When a soldier marches, his uniform is not the army; it is a sign and symbol of the army under whose command he serves. So it is with the ordinance of baptism. It is not the instrument of change; rather, it is a sign and symbol of the commitment that a man has made in his heart and life.

This is evident throughout the pages of the New Testament. In Acts 8, Philip, guided by the Holy Spirit, is sent to the Ethiopian treasurer who is reading from Isaiah. As the Ethiopian reads, Philip asks, "Do you understand what you are reading?" The man replies, "How could I except a man guide me?" He was pondering this passage,

> All we like sheep have gone astray; we have turned every one to his own way; and the LORD hath laid on him the iniquity of us all.
>
> He was oppressed, and he was afflicted, yet he opened not his mouth: he is brought as a lamb to the slaughter, and as a sheep before her shearers is dumb, so he openeth not his mouth (Is. 53:6–7).

The account in Acts 8 continues,

> Then Philip opened his mouth, and began at the same scripture, and preached unto him Jesus.
>
> And as they went out on their way, they came unto a certain water: and the eunuch said, See, here is water; what doth hinder me to be baptized? [He understood baptism as a sign of the change in a man's heart—the acceptance of our Lord.]
>
> And Philip said, If thou believest with all thine heart, thou mayest. And he answered and said, I believe that Jesus Christ is the Son of God.
>
> And he commanded the chariot to stand still: and they went down both into the water, both Philip and the eunuch; and he baptized him.
>
> And when they were come up out of the water, the Spirit of the Lord caught away Philip, that the eunuch saw him no more: and he went on his way rejoicing (Acts 8:35–39).

When a man meets the Lord and is saved, the first desire in his heart is for baptism. I cannot imagine a hungry man who would not want to eat. I cannot think of a thirsty man who does not want a drink. I cannot conceive of a cold man who does not want to be warm. Nor can I think of a saved man who does not want to be baptized. Baptism symbolizes our death to the world and our resurrection to a new life in Christ. It symbolizes our obedience to the Savior who died for our sins.

Jesus came to John and said "I want to be baptized," so that He might identify Himself with us who are lost sinners. Every apostle was baptized by John the Baptist in order to qualify to be an apostle.

> And Ananias went his way, and entered into the house; and putting his hands on him said, Brother Saul, the Lord, even Jesus, that appeared unto thee in the way thou camest, hath sent me, that thou mightest receive thy sight, and be filled with the Holy Ghost.
> And immediately there fell from his eyes as it had been scales: and he received sight forthwith, and arose, and was baptized (Acts 9:17–18).

In Acts 2 we read:

> Now when they heard this, they were pricked in their heart, and said unto Peter and to the rest of the apostles, Men and brethren, what shall we do?
> Then Peter said unto them, Repent, and be baptized every one of you in the name of Jesus Christ for [*eis*, meaning "because of"] the remission of sins . . . (Acts 2:37–38).

Baptism is the first ordinance; it is the rite of obedience; it is the ceremony of testimony for us who have found new life in Christ. The new dispensation began with that ordinance, and the new experience we have in accepting Christ begins with that ordinance. That is the beginning of our new life.

FINDING EVANGELISTIC POWER

In those strange and unusual providences of the Lord, He inherently placed in that ordinance a powerful witness for Christ. It is dynamically evangelistic.

In the first chapter of the Gospel of John, the religious leaders asked John the Baptist, "Where did you get that authority and why do you baptize?" He replied,

> And I knew him not: but that he should be made manifest to Israel, therefore am I come baptizing with water.
> And John bare record, saying, I saw the Spirit descending from heaven like a dove, and it abode upon him.

> And I knew him not: but he that sent me to baptize with water,
> the same said unto me, Upon whom thou shalt see the Spirit de-
> scending, and remaining on him, the same is he which baptizeth
> with the Holy Ghost.
> And I saw, and bare record that this is the Son of God (vv.
> 31–34).

John declares that the purpose of his baptizing is to manifest Jesus to Israel and to the world. The purpose of the ordinance is evangelistic. It is to lift up Christ and bring men to Him.

You see that in the Great Commission. In the heart of that mandate discipling and baptizing are together. Make disciples; win them to Jesus, baptizing them. It is God's way of building up His kingdom and extending the evangelistic outreach of His church. Baptism is an instrument and vehicle with inherent power of witnessing to salvation.

My father used to tell me about the raids of the Commanche Indians in Texas. I can hardly believe that my father lived during those days. I fervently remember listening as a boy to those old frontier preachers out in the western part of the state. Some of the things those pioneer preachers told about are as indelibly inscribed in my soul as though they were burned in my memory with a hot iron. What a price those preachers paid to deliver the message of Jesus!

In the days of the rugged pioneers in Texas, a preacher won to the Lord and to the faith the beautiful and precious wife of a vile, rough, and wicked man. When the day came for her baptism, the man said, "If the preacher baptizes my wife, I will beat him to death with a rawhide whip"—a "black snake," as we called it. The baptismal day came, and the preacher was in the water with a Bible in his hand, preaching the gospel of the grace of the Son of God. Then he came to the edge of the water and they sang a song, "Jesus, I my cross have taken, all I leave to follow Thee."

Mary, the beautiful wife of that rough and wicked man came to the edge of the water, dressed in white and ready to be baptized. Leaping out of his buggy, her vile husband, with his long bullwhip, made his way to the front. The precious wife entered the water, walked out to meet the pastor and was lowered into the watery grave and then raised up into a new life in Christ. The crowd, who had gathered there from all around the area to see the preacher whipped, gasped when she came to the edge of the water, but the bullwhip somehow seemed to loose itself from the hand of that vile and wicked man, and it fell to the ground. He lifted his wife Mary into his arms and carried her to the buggy. Then turning back, he came to the edge of the water and said to the pastor, "I ask you to forgive me. I ask God to forgive me. I have repented, and I accept Jesus as my Lord, and I want to be baptized."

You might think that is very unusual, but another incident happened in my own first pastorate. We called the place Burt Hollow. The old patriarch, Will Burt, together with his large family and his brothers and their families, lived there. I visited and prayed and pleaded with these hard and harsh men to come to Christ. Preaching under an arbor at the end of a revival, I was baptizing my converts in the Leon River. As I always did, I stood out in the middle of the stream with my open Bible and preached to the throngs on either side. Then after I preached, standing out there in the middle of the water, I came to the water's edge and made an appeal for Christ. We always sang,

> Happy day, happy day,
> When Jesus washed my sins away!
> He taught me how to watch and pray
> And live rejoicing every day;
> Happy day, happy day,
> When Jesus washed my sins away!

This was my invitation. As I stood there on the banks of the water, down through the throng came Will Burt and his family and his brothers and their families saying, "Pastor, we want to be baptized. We have found the Lord. We have given our hearts to Jesus."

Inherently in the ordinance is a witness for Christ that is beautiful and precious and powerful. I remember my own baptismal service as though it were yesterday, and yet that was more than sixty years ago. We begin our Christian life with a testimony of what Jesus has done for us in raising us out of the old life of death and despair and opening for us the doors of hope and of glory.

8

The Memorial Supper

There are four accounts of the institution of the Lord's Supper in the New Testament: Matthew 26:26–29; Mark 14:22–24; Luke 22:19–20; 1 Corinthians 11:23–26.

THE HISTORICAL SETTING FOR THE MEMORIAL SUPPER

The subject of the memorial supper is always introduced as though it belonged to one of the most solemn hours in the life of our Lord. Matthew, Mark, and Luke introduced it as they were eating the Passover, the most meaningful and significant sacred observance in the life of Israel. Always the ordinance is written and presented in the framework of deepest solemnity.

The apostle Paul introduces the ordinance in this way:

> For I have received of the Lord that which also I delivered unto you [i.e., by direct revelation from Christ Himself rather than by the mediation of an apostle], That the Lord Jesus the same night in which he was betrayed took bread (1 Cor. 11:23a).

In Galatians he presents the institution of this holy ordinance:

> But when it pleased God, who separated me from my mother's womb, and called me by his grace,
> To reveal his Son in me, that I might preach him among the heathen; immediately I conferred not with flesh and blood:
> Neither went I up to Jerusalem to them which were apostles before me; but I went into Arabia, and returned again unto Damascus (1:15–17).

78

In the three years of Paul's preparation, Christ personally revealed to him the gospel he was to preach. He received his instruction by direct revelation from Christ Himself.

During the Passover our Lord took unleavened bread that was made out of crushed ground wheat flour mixed with water and baked it in the fire. The bread was unleavened during the first Passover that was shared by the families of Israel on that dark night in Egypt when the death angel passed over. In the lament and cry of all Egypt over the death of their first-born, the children of Israel were thrust out of the land of captivity. There was no time to knead the bread. There was no time to leaven it. There was no time for the bread to rise. There was time only to take the flour, mix it with water, put it in the fire, and then hurriedly leave the land of slavery and bondage. Therefore, this *matzo* is unleavened.

Also, the bread is unleavened because universally in the Bible leaven is a symbol and a type of sin. When the Lord says "This is my body," that bread could not have leaven in it because the life of our Savior was without sin or fault, perfect in every way.

While the Lord was eating the Passover with His disciples, He took the *matzo,* broke it, and gave a broken piece of the unleavened bread to each one of the disciples.

> And when he had given thanks, he brake it, and said, Take, eat: this is my body, which is broken for you: this do in remembrance of me.
>
> After the same manner also he took the cup, when he had supped, saying, This cup is the new testament [compact, promise, covenant] in my blood: this do ye, as oft as ye drink it, in remembrance of me (1 Cor. 11:24–25).

In the solemnity of that hour, Jesus pointed to Judas as the one who would betray Him. Then followed those beautiful discourses written in John 14 through 16, the High Priestly Prayer written in John 17, and in all of the Gospels an account of the agony of Gethsemane, of our Lord's arrest and trial by the Sanhedrin, of His trial by the Roman court before the procurator Pontius Pilate, and finally of His suffering and crucifixion on the cross. The memorial supper is set in the most solemn, sacred, and deeply meaningful moments in the life of our Lord.

It is a tragedy unspeakable and indescribable that this simple meal of eating bread and drinking the cup should be the center of the bitterest confrontations and controversies in the history of the Christian church. The meal is plain and simple—bread and the fruit of the vine—as though it had been drawn by an angel's hand. It is so easily understood that a child can look upon it in reverence and wonder, and yet it is a center of implacable strife.

The Roman Catholics developed the doctrine of transubstantiation. *Trans,* the Latin word for "change," is combined with *substantia,* meaning "substance." Thus, transubstantiation suggests that the bread and the cup are transferred or changed into the actual body and blood of Christ.

Again during the Reformation came the Lutheran Church's doctrine called by historians consubstantiation. *Con,* the Latin word for "with," explains the doctrine as meaning "with the substance." The bread and the cup do not actually turn into the body and blood of Jesus under the hand of the priest, but the actual presence—i.e., the body and the blood—are present with the bread and the cup.

The Reformed, Calvinist church under John Calvin developed still another interpretation. They maintained that the bodily presence of Christ is not in blood and flesh but that He is dynamically present spiritually.

Finally, Zwingli appeared on the scene to teach that the elements are but symbolic presentations representing the body and the blood of Christ.

However the doctrine has been presented, it has been bitterly fought, defended, and denounced. Our Lord's simple meal has become a struggle of corrosion and differentiation and a theological battleground through the centuries of the history of the church. How tragic this is in light of the simple presentation of this eucharistic celebration in Scripture.

The Administration of the Memorial Supper

The Lord's Supper is set in the heart of the church. It is neither a feast nor a supper that belongs to the congress or the legislature or the judiciary or the civic club. It is peculiarly and unusually a church ordinance.

The order of the memorial supper is plainly and simply presented in the Great Commission.

The Memorial Supper

Go ye therefore, and teach [make disciples of] all nations, baptizing them in the name of the Father, and of the Son, and of the Holy Ghost:

Teaching them to observe all things whatsoever I have commanded you . . . (Matt. 28:19–20).

The order is clear. First, we are to be saved by accepting the Lord as Savior. Second, we are to be baptized—buried with our Lord and raised to walk with Him in newness of life.

We are to keep this holy ordinance as He delivered it to us by breaking bread and drinking the cup. The order is as inspired as the content: I am to be saved, I am to be baptized as He was in the Jordan River and as He commands me to be a follower of Him, and I am to break bread and drink the cup.

The Scriptures are no less plain to us regarding the elements of the Lord's Supper. They are two: the *matzo* or unleavened bread and the cup or fruit of the vine. It is a very interesting thing to me as I study the Scriptures that at no time in the four accounts of the institution of the Lord's Supper is the word "wine" used. Always it is called the "cup" or the "fruit of the vine."

Canning—the keeping of a liquid such as grape juice or food like fruits or vegetables—was not invented until A.D. 1800. It was discovered by Napoleon's army. In order to conquer the world, Napoleon had to feed his troops, and thus he was responsible for the introduction to the world of the canning process, which permitted food to be protected from spoiling by its being placed in a vacuum.

The Lord knew all about that, and back in that day long ago when there was no possibility of keeping crushed fruit of the vine without its fermenting, the Lord knew this day was coming, and He purposefully never used the word "wine" but instead "cup" or "fruit of the vine."

Once I attended a service in which they pinched off pieces of light bread and served water to observe the memorial supper. I cannot describe how I felt, but I do know that it is far better for us to follow the Holy Scriptures. Let us take unleavened bread and the crushed fruit of the vine as the Bible says and eat and drink the simple meal as directed by our Lord.

The Scripture does not give a specific directive as to when and how often we are to take the Lord's Supper.

81

> For as often as ye eat this bread, and drink this cup, ye do show
> the Lord's death till he come (1 Cor. 11:26).

In Acts 2, the Lord's Supper was observed every day. In Troas, the believers observed it on Sunday (Acts 20). The frequency of its observance is left to us. I would not object to having the Lord's Supper in the sanctuary of our church every day. Those who would come at any hour of the day and break bread and share the cup would be beautifully in order. I would not object to our observing the Lord's Supper every week. However, in our church we observe it once a month. In the little churches that I pastored when I was a young minister, we observed it every quarter. It is left to the congregation. The Scripture says that as often as we do it, we are to do it in remembrance of Him.

The Scriptures have another admonishment for us concerning the Lord's Supper. We are to come into its presence with deepest soul-searching. It is to be presented in reverence and received with self-examination.

> But let a man examine himself, and so let him eat of that bread,
> and drink of that cup.
> For he that eateth and drinketh unworthily, eateth and drinketh
> damnation to himself, not discerning the Lord's body (1 Cor.
> 11:28–29).

Not one of us is worthy. We would never be able to approach the Lord's Table if it were dependent upon our worthiness. In Corinth they were gormandizing at the love feast, and they were drinking until they were sot drunk. That is why Paul is writing to them. Thus to observe the Lord's Supper in an unworthy manner, according to Paul, is to eat and drink judgment to yourself.

Then the apostle adds a sentence that to me is one of the most unusual in the Bible.

> For this cause [because of the way you observe the Lord's
> Supper] many are weak and sickly among you, and many sleep [i.e.,
> they are dead] (1 Cor. 11:30).

In keeping with the solemnity of Christ, the way in which many do not reverence this holy ordinance has caused weakness and illness and even death. God help us to administer the things of Christ worthily, in a precious, beautiful, and spiritually appropriate way.

The Memorial Supper

THE BIBLICAL MEANING OF THE MEMORIAL SUPPER

There are several meanings that are plainly written here in the Word of God. First, it is a memorial to the atoning death of our Savior. "This do in remembrance of me," and they ate a piece of bread; "This do in remembrance of me," and they drank from the cup. It brings back to our minds and memories the sufferings of our Lord for our sins, lest we forget.

There are many kinds of memorials on the earth. If you have ever been in Washington, D.C., you have seen there a tall, monolithic marble monument to the Father of our country—the Washington Monument. In Egypt, you can see many towering obelisks.

Sometimes a monument will take the form of a mausoleum. In India, you will see the most beautiful mausoleum in the world—the Taj Mahal—build by Shah Jahan in memory of a beloved wife.

But our Lord did not create a monument out of marble to bring to us the memory of our Savior's suffering in our behalf. In fact, this memorial is not in the form of any kind of structure. He did it in a primeval, fundamental, and basic way—by eating and drinking—and this simple memorial is to be repeated again and again and again. The broken bread recalls for us His torn body, and the crimson of the cup reminds us of the blood poured out upon the earth for the remission of our sins.

First, then, it is a memorial—"This do in remembrance of me"—to bring back to our minds and hearts the atoning sacrifice of our Lord.

Second, in all four accounts it is described as the new covenant, the new compact, the new promise, the new testament.

How is this covenant new or different? The old covenant was the law. On page after page the law says "do this and live." According to Exodus 24:7, Moses took the book of the covenant and read it to Israel. The Ten Commandments were placed in an ark called the ark of the covenant. You had to obey the law in order to live.

But who among us can obey the law? How could I ever stand before the Lord and say, "Lord, I have loved Thee with all of my heart and all of my mind and all of my strength amd all of my soul, and I have never deviated from that devotion to Thee."

83

Who could ever say that? The law condemns us. The law reveals to us our depravity and our sin. That is the old covenant.

The new covenant says, "Trust and be saved. Believe and your sins are washed away." The new covenant rests upon the sacrificial, atoning death of our Lord. I am not perfect but He was. I face the penalty of judgment and death, but He died for me. The righteousness of God found in Him by imputation has been credited to my account. When I stand before God, I can say, "Lord, I am not worthy, but He is. I am not sinless, but He is. I do not deserve an entrance into God's heaven, but He opened the door for me, and I stand in His grace and love."

This leads to the third symbolic aspect of the supper. In all four accounts it is called a "eucharist." He took bread and *eucharisteō,* meaning "to give thanks," and He took the cup and *eucharisteō.* It is thus a thanksgiving feast. It is the expression of our gratitude to God for saving us from our sins.

The age in which we live is a part of all of us. We reflect the times and the generation in which our lives and lots are cast. All of us bring this influence into the church and into our religious experience. We cannot help it. We are a part of the church in this generation and consequently bring a part of that age into the church. We are taught, and rightly so, that in this life and age we strive and struggle for everything—excellence, affluence, success, fame, advancement. We are taught that if you do not strive for these things, you are looked upon as lazy, immature, trifling, or a parasite. I can well understand how we somehow unconsciously believe that a man ought to strive and struggle for achievement and excellence. The problem arises when we bring that into our religion and into our faith, unconsciously falling into the false doctrine that if one is to be saved, he must struggle for that salvation. Salvation is then something that *I* do. *I* win it. It is a matter of my works and effort.

To my sorrow many of the great denominations of Christendom believe that salvation is dependent upon works, a matter of doing good, the result of striving and struggling and grasping. Consequently, these religious pilgrims never find rest in their hearts. How does one know whether he is good enough or whether he has run the race well enough or whether he has ever achieved enough? You never know whether you are saved or lost if your salvation depends upon you and your good works.

84

The Memorial Supper

The memorial supper is a denial of all human effort. The supper is an announcement from God that our salvation is not a matter of our good works or our worth, but our salvation is a matter of our acceptance. It is a matter of looking in faith and trust to the Lord Jesus and taking salvation from His gracious hands.

> Not by works of righteousness which we have done, but according to his mercy he saved us . . . (Titus 3:5).

> For by grace are ye saved through faith; and that not of yourselves: it is the gift of God:
> Not of works, lest any man should boast (Eph. 2:8–9).

That is proclaimed in all four accounts of the memorial supper. The first word the Lord utters is "take" (*lambanō,* meaning "to receive," "to take"). The verb is second aorist imperative. There is no one of us who has ever participated in the Lord's Supper but that we take the bread from the hands of another. There is no one of us who ever shared the Lord's Supper but that we take the cup from the hands of somebody else. The first words are "take and eat" or "take and drink." The Christian life does not begin in a struggle or in a personal effort or in an attempt to be worthy. The Christian life begins in a confession, in a believing acceptance, in a trusting, receiving. "Believe on the Lord Jesus Christ, accept Him in all of His atoning grace, and you shall be saved."

The Christian life is not one of strife and struggle to enter heaven, but it is a pilgrim way of expressing gratitude to God for the blood He shed for me. Indeed, the Christian life is proclaimed in that simple meal. We sing of it in one of our great hymns.

> Could my tears forever flow,
> Could my zeal no languor know,
> This for sin could not atone—
> Thou must save, and Thou alone:
> In my hand no price I bring,
> Simply to Thy cross I cling.

We are saved by the blood of the crucified One. We receive salvation as a gift from His nail-pierced hands as we take the bread, His broken body, and as we take the cup, the crimson of His life.

Fourth, it is also a *koinōnia,* a beautiful word from the Greek New Testament.

> The cup of blessing which we bless, is it not the communion [*koinōnia*] of the blood of Christ? The bread which we break, is it not the communion [*koinōnia*] of the body of Christ? (1 Cor. 10:16).

Koinōnia may be translated "fellowship" or "communion" or "relationship" or "sharing." This supper is a communion, a relationship, a sharing with Jesus our Lord.

Our relationship, our *koinōnia,* in the Christian faith is not with impersonal law. It is not with two cold tables of stone nor even with Mount Sinai that was split and torn and shaken with thunder and lightning in the presence of the holiness and judgment of almighty God so much so that even if an animal touched the mountain it died. Moses cried saying, "I do exceedingly fear and tremble," and the people fled away saying, "Let us not see God or hear His voice." Our relationship is not with law and judgment. Rather, our relationship is with Mt. Zion, with an innumerable host of angels, with the spirits of just men made perfect, with the New Jerusalem, and with the blood of Christ that speaks beautiful and precious things for us. That is this memorial, the *koinōnia,* our relationship with Christ. It is one of praise and thanksgiving for what He has done for me.

Fifth, it is a feeding upon our Lord for daily strength. Following are words in the Bible which, when spoken, caused all the disciples to leave Jesus.

> Then Jesus said unto them, Verily, verily, I say unto you, Except ye eat the flesh of the Son of man, and drink his blood, ye have no life in you.
> Whoso eateth my flesh, and drinketh my blood, hath eternal life; and I will raise him up at the last day.
> For my flesh is meat indeed, and my blood is drink indeed.
> He that eateth my flesh, and drinketh my blood, dwelleth in me, and I in him.
> As the living Father hath sent me, and I live by the Father: so he that eateth me, even he shall live by me.
> This is that bread which came down from heaven: not as your fathers did eat manna, and are dead: he that eateth of this bread shall live forever (John 6:53–58).

No wonder those followers of Jesus turned aside and said, "How could a man believe or accept such a thing as this?" But for us who are taught in the faith, it becomes a beautiful pilgrimage. As in baptism we are buried and raised to walk in a new life, so in this recurring church ordinance we are taught to feed upon this manna, the angel's food that comes down from heaven. We are to feed upon Christ—every day in His word and in prayer with our hearts opened heavenward, Christward, and Godward. We find strength in our daily sharing of this manna from heaven.

Sixth, this supper is a prophetic eschatalogical promise and hope. All of the accounts are very careful to present that.

> But I say unto you, I will not drink henceforth of this fruit of the vine, until that day when I drink it new with you in my Father's kingdom (Matt. 26:29).

The next time Jesus will bless the cup and share it with us will be when we sit down at the marriage supper of the Lamb. Paul writes of it this way:

> For as often as ye eat this bread, and drink this cup, ye do show the Lord's death till he come (1 Cor. 11:26).

It is an eschatalogical, prophetic promise of the messianic day when Jesus Himself shall feed us.

Lord, will there ever be a day when God makes everything that is wrong right! Will He ever intervene in human history so that we do not learn war anymore and cease to build atomic bombs to destroy our fellowmen and no longer hate, kill, rob, and terrorize? Is there ever such a day coming? This supper is a promise of that wonderful coming day. Eating bread and drinking the fruit of the vine is an overt act on our part to express our confident hope that someday Jesus is coming again.

As it looks to the past in memory—His death for us—as it portrays the present—feeding on the manna from heaven, even so it looks to the future when Jesus shall sit down with us in the kingdom of the Father. The supper encompasses all time, all revelation, all Christian experience, and every hope and promise we have in Christ.

9

The Jesus of the Memorial Supper

For I have received of the Lord that which also I delivered unto you, That the Lord Jesus the same night in which he was betrayed took bread:

And when he had given thanks, he brake it, and said, Take, eat: this is my body which is broken for you: this do in remembrance of me.

After the same manner also he took the cup, when he had supped, saying, This cup is the new testament in my blood: this do ye, as oft as ye drink it, in remembrance of me.

For as often as ye eat this bread, and drink this cup, ye do show the Lord's death till he come (1 Cor. 11:23–26).

A PORTRAIT OF JESUS AT NIGHT

Paul first mentions here a nighttime portrait of our Lord: ". . . the *same* night in which he was betrayed took bread." Against the dark background of the midnight, the apostle draws the curtain aside and lets us see our Master as He is at night. A man can be one person in the blazing light of public gaze and in the stark reality of the sunlight. But he can be an altogether different person under the cover of evening, in the darkness of the watches of the night.

Jesus is like God the Father. How marvelously does He appear at night. In Psalms 8 and 19, the heavens present, publish, and declare [*katangellō*] the glory of God. We see His lacework and handiwork in the stars of the firmament. "By night an atheist is half a believer in God." It was in the nighttime that the Lord appeared to Israel in a pillar of fire. It was in the nighttime that the Lord came to Solomon with the words that all of us memorized in childhood:

> If my people, which are called by my name, shall humble them-
> selves, and pray, and seek my face, and turn from their wicked
> ways; then will I hear from heaven, and will forgive their sin, and will
> heal their land (2 Chr. 7:14).

It was in the nighttime that the Lord appeared to the prophet-statesman Daniel and in chapters 2 and 7 of that prophetic book unveiled the future course of humanity down to the consummation of the age.

When the curtain is drawn back and we see our Lord as He is at night, He is the same wonderful Savior. The Bible says that He prayed all night. The Scriptures say that at night He came to His disciples walking on the stormy sea. In the week of His passion, He taught in the temple in the daytime, and at night He abode on the Mount of Olives communing with His Father.

This is the last night in His mortal flesh. How does He spend it, and what is He like? He spends the time with His apostles. He is assuring them in comforting words, "Let not your heart be troubled. I will not leave you comfortless." He spends the night in thanksgiving to God, singing psalms and saying words of encouragement and endearment, praying the High Priestly Prayer, and finally assuring His disciples of His coming return.

THE UNUSUAL SENTENCE OF PAUL

Look again as Paul writes of our Lord:

> . . . the Lord Jesus the same night in which he was betrayed
> took bread (1 Cor. 11:23).

That is a most unusual indication—"the same night in which he was betrayed." He could have written "the night of the Passover" since He was eating that memorial supper when the Lord's Supper was given to us. Or, why not say "the night in which He washed the apostles' feet"? Or why not say "the night when He prayed in Gethsemane"? Why not say "the night He was arrested and turned over to the Romans"? Why not write "the night He was tried before the Sanhedrin and before Pontius Pilate"? Why not write "the night before He was crucified"? Why does he write "the same night in which he was betrayed"?

Could it be that the apostle is not so much writing down a

89

date and a time as he is presenting a portrait of our tender and loving Lord against the dark background of a traitorous betrayal. In the presence of incarnate sin (John says that Satan entered into Judas), the loving Lord prepares and spreads this table of grace and blessing—"in the same night in which he was betrayed."

Against that dark background of his betrayal, Paul painted the loving picture of our Lord in clear and distinct tones. Perhaps it is like a Rembrandt portrait. I have seen those Rembrandts in great galleries and museums all over this world, and they all are painted alike. They are painted with vivid contrast of light and color. Rembrandt would paint a dark background black, and then the face of the individual in such bold relief that the features of the face would stand out with an intense light against that dark black background.

It seems to me that this is the same kind of portrait Paul is painting here of our dear Lord—"the same night in which he was betrayed." On that treacherous, traitorous, heinous, black night, we see our Lord unveil the ordinance of grace and love that saves us from our sins.

The reaction of the apostles concerning the betrayal of Judas was bitter and hostile. For example, the name of Judas appears twenty times and more in the story, and every time without exception it is followed by that epithet, "Judas, the one who betrayed Him." He is never mentioned except as "the one who betrayed him." Judas was one of the Twelve. He had followed the footsteps of the Master all through the years of His public ministry. He seemingly was the most trusted member of the group. He was the treasurer, as John noted—"he had the bag." He was loved. For him Jesus prayed and hoped, and he was taught in the ways of our dear Lord.

The revulsion of the apostles to what Judas did is quite understandable. Had a Pharisee conspired with Herod to deliver Jesus to death, had a Sadducee conspired with Caiaphas to deliver Him to death, had a publican conspired with a Roman soldier to divide the silver and deliver him to death, it might have been understandable, but not for one of His inner circle to betray Him.

Look at the response of our blessed Lord. You would think that, in the presence of the betrayer, the Lord would give Himself to a vituperative floodtide of loathing or of stinging rebuke or maybe of cursing as He had just cursed the fig tree so that it withered away. You would think there would have been some tone or gesture of denunciation in the voice and words of our Lord.

He had watched Judas all through the years. In John 6 when the people tried to make Jesus a king, it was Judas whom the Lord pointed out as the devil who was to betray Him. When Mary of Bethany broke the alabaster box, it was Judas who said in his covetousness (even John called him a thief), "Why was it not sold? It would bring a year's wages." Jesus knew all and watched it unfold until the climax—like a chemist observing an experiment to its consummation or a physician watching the course of a disease to its fever. You would think that Jesus would have said some word of imprecation and denunciation in the presence of so vile and heinous a deed.

A portrait of Jesus against the background of darkness— what did He do? At the same time the traitor was dipping the sop with Him in the dish, Jesus was instituting the memorial for His remission of our sins. At the same time the traitor was watching for the moment to go and meet his fellow conspirators and de- liver Jesus to them, the Savior was breaking bread by his side.

Our finite minds cannot understand the gentle Savior.When our Lord pointed Judas out and gave him the sop, He spoke so kindly and graciously to the traitor that all of the other apostles—except Peter and John, who knew what Jesus was doing—thought that the Lord was saying to Judas, "Remember the poor; give something to the poor." At that same time the most the Lord said to Judas was, "What you do, do quickly." It was as you would speak to an executioner with his axe raised, "Make it soon."

When He was betrayed, all the Lord said to Judas was, "My friend, do you betray your Lord with a kiss?" This is the portrait of our Lord against so dark a background—"the same night in which he was betrayed."

As I read about and study the abounding grace of God that covers our sins, I am overwhelmed. It was thus also in the Gar- den of Eden when our first parents fell and the Lord covered their transgression with His grace, mercy, and love. It was so in the parable of the prophet Hosea. When his wife left him to become a prostitute and finally was sold into slavery, under the commandment of God, Hosea lovingly and tenderly bought her back and restored her as his wife. God covers our sins with His grace.

When Simon Peter cursed and swore saying, "I never saw Him; I do not know Him," the Lord turned to him in agony of soul. When next He spoke to Peter, Jesus simply said, "Simon, son of Jonah, lovest thou me?"

Saul of Tarsus, breathing out threatening and slaughter against the people of God, was on the way to Damascus to haul the followers of Jesus into prison and on to death. The Lord met him in the way; He could have lashed out at Saul, "You damnable traitor to the truth and revelation of God for whom the fires of judgment and hell are reserved!" Does He say that? No. When He stops the bitter, vengeful Saul of Tarsus in the way, He says, "Saul, Saul, why persecutest thou me?" Saul replies, "Who art thou, Lord?" Does the Lord say, "I am the great, omnipotent, all-powerful almighty who is ready to cast you down into damnation?" No. He simply says, "I am Jesus of Nazareth." The human Jesus, who was born of a virgin, who worked in his father's carpenter shop, and who went about doing good—this was His most humble title.

THE MEMORIAL JESUS INSTITUTED

Notice once again how the Lord evaluates what is important in His life and ministry and in His mission on earth by the unusual memorial He institutes.

"This is my body broken, eat in remembrance of me. This is my blood poured out, drink in remembrance of me." The memorial is of His death. We are different in that we memorialize by placing all of our rejoicing, activities, and remembrances on birthdays. We have a national remembrance on Washington's birthday. Some states celebrate Lincoln's birthday. There is a vast effort on the part of the black community of America to make the birthday of Martin Luther King, Jr., a national holiday. This is our custom and pleasure. I am invited world without end to parties and dinners celebrating a birthday, but I have never yet been invited to any kind of party or dinner celebrating the anniversary of somebody's death. Yet our Lord instituted a memorial to His death.

When you read the Scriptures, you will find many memorials in the Bible. In Exodus 12, the Passover is a memorial to the deliverance of the people of Israel out of bondage. In that same book of Exodus, God tells Moses to write a book and make sure Joshua learns about it, for it is to be a memorial to destroy the enemies of the Lord. Another memorial described in Exodus is one in which onyx stones are placed on the shoulders of the high priest, and on them are the names of the twelve tribes of Israel for a memorial before God to remember His people.

The Book of Joshua notes that when the Israelites crossed the Jordan River, they took twelve stones and set them on the other side in Gilgal for a memorial of when Israel passed over into the Promised Land at the miracle of the parting of the Jordan River.

When Mary of Bethany broke the alabaster box, Jesus promised that wherever the gospel would be preached this would be told as a memorial to her.

The alms of the Roman Centurion Cornelius had risen to God as a memorial in His presence, according to the angel in Acts 10. There are all kinds of memorials, but not one like this—the memorial of a death, the death of our Lord. It shows us how Jesus evaluated His life and ministry and the purpose for which He came to the earth.

Jesus did not say, "Make me a mighty mausoleum to mark my last resting place." He did not say, "Erect here a tall marble column where I delivered the Sermon on the Mount." Nor did He say, "Make me a memorial of a marble granite cenotaph where I fed the five thousand." He did say, "This bread and this cup memorialize my death for you for the remission of sins." The supper is a portrait of our Lord Himself. That memorial was, is, and shall be in countless millions of human hearts yesterday, today, and, according to the promise, until Jesus shall come again.

Jesus never led a conquering army. He never subdued a mighty empire. He never did anything that had any vestige or facet or overture of greatness or fame or achievement in the judgment of the comtemporary world in which He lived. There is not one contemporary historian who mentions the Lord Jesus. They are consumed with the Caesars in Rome or with the Herods in Palestine or with the Greek games or the Roman conquests, but they never referred to Jesus. And yet today He is enshrined in our hearts forever.

There are humanists and atheists who are doing everything in their power to take the name of Jesus out of the public schools, away from public prayer, and even to disassociate Christ from Christmas. But you will never do it. To destroy the name of Jesus from our memories you would have to destroy the best literature and the greatest music and the finest art. You would have to destroy our very laws and the foundation of our western civilization. Christ is memorialized in our hearts in love and worship and gratitude forever and ever.

The Proclamation of the Gospel
in the Memorial of His Death

"For as often as you eat this bread, and drink this cup, ye do show the Lord's death till he come." The Greek words translated "show" *(katangellō)* means "publicize," "openly declare," "preach," "proclaim the gospel message of our Lord." Even in this last memorial institution and ordinance, the Lord has our salvation in His heart and mind.

There are many ways of preaching the gospel. It may be done in the pulpit. In years gone by, I used to stand on the street corner and in a courthouse square and preach the gospel. We preach the gospel by personal testimony, "My brother, I have found the gospel, come and welcome." We proclaim the gospel by singing, by invitation, by religious literature—a tract, a brochure, a pamphlet—by our holy living, by our giving tithes and offerings, and by the media on radio and television. Jesus says that this memorial supper is a way of proclaiming, preaching, publicly declaring, openly demonstrating, dramatizing the gospel. This ordinance of the breaking of bread and the drinking of the cup becomes a universal language. It speaks to the human heart.

Once when I preached in the Moscow Baptist Church, I was invited to share in presiding over the Lord's Table. I could not understand a word of the service, but I was moved in my heart as I shared the broken bread and the fruit of the vine with those dear oppressed people. It is a universal language. I have shared that same ordinance in Germany, Italy, Australia, and around this earth. Though I could not understand a word in many of the places, I was deeply moved in my heart.

The ordinance involves a universal experience—eating and drinking. We could not live without food and drink, nor as Christians could we survive without the manna from heaven and the blood that washes our sins away. How plain and simple to eat and to drink, and our Lord says that this is His gospel.

One of our great pastors was dying in London, England. His brethren gathered around him and said, "Do you have one last word for the world?" He replied, "I do. Oh, preacher, make it plain how a man can be saved."

It is a fallen and depraved nature that causes the theologian to make our salvation a matter of philosophical, metaphysical speculation. God made it plain. It is always to eat and to drink. It is to look and live. It is to believe and be saved. It is to wash and be clean. Always it is a plain, humble, simple way—so plain that a wayfaring man need not err in it; so simple that a stranger passing by need not miss the way. The loving invitation of our Lord is, "Come and dine, come and be saved, come and find eternal life."

How grateful I am that it was plain enough for me as a ten-year-old boy to find the way. I was no theologian; but as a child, I could believe and accept in my heart, and I did.

Except we all become as children and thus come into the kingdom, we are in no way able to enter. I do not appear before God in brilliance or excellence, in my own worth, or in my own knowledge or understanding. I appear before God saying, "God, be good to me. Help me. Be merciful to me and may Thy saving grace cover my sins and live in my heart and soul forever."

10

The Ordained Officers of the Church

> Paul and Timothy, the servants of Jesus Christ, to all the saints in Christ Jesus which are at Philippi, with the bishops and deacons (Phil. 1:1).

Paul identifies the two ordained officers in the organized life of the church as bishops and deacons. We shall first discuss what they have in common and then the unique assignments of each.

What They Share in Common

There are five characteristics of the pastor and deacon presented in the Bible.

Leadership. The pastor and deacon make up the leadership of the church. If you read a harmony of the gospels or a harmony of the life of Christ, you will find that as He began to meet difficulty and opposition in His public ministry, He ordained, called out, set aside, and gave authority to twelve apostles and sent them out to preach the message of redemption. It is thus in the church. In the imperfect, fallen world in which the Lord has placed His church, an effective leadership is essential for the church to be strong. That leadership is provided in the two ordained officers of the church—the pastor and deacons.

Spiritual Qualifications. In 1 Timothy 3, Paul lists the qualifications of a pastor, and then he begins the eighth verse with the Greek word *hosautos,* meaning "in the same way" and translated here "likewise." These are the spiritual qualifications:

(1) Publicly both officers are to receive a good report. They

are to be men of integrity and are to be known as such beyond the church in the community. There must be public acknowledgement of blameless ethical character.

(2) Domestically, they are interdicted from being polygamous or deuterogamous; rather they must be monogamous. Though Paul lived in a day when many men had more than one wife, an officer of the church was to have only one wife. Of course, a man would be foolish to try to support two of them financially in our day!.

(3) Spiritually, they are to hold the mystery of the faith in a pure conscience. The minister of Christ, of course, is to be a man who cares for the flock in feeding them, preaching to them, and being responsible to God for their souls. What you expect of the pastor, according to God's Book, you are also to expect of the deacons.

Spiritual Examination. No man is to be ordained without first being carefully tried and tested.

> Lay hands suddenly [*tacheos,* meaning "hastily" or "quickly"] on no man, neither be partaker of other men's sins: keep thyself pure (1 Tim. 5:22).

In my first little congregation I had eighteen members. I began preaching and pastoring when I was a teenager. I had read in the Bible that we were to have deacons in the church, and I was determined to obey that biblical injunction and ordain deacons. We chose three deacons to be ordained. When the time for ordination came, one of them was drunk, and he was not there. The other one was so sorry that he did not show up. We ordained the third one, and he soon fell away. That was the result of my adolescent immaturity as a young and inexperienced pastor.

In years past our church has ordained men to the ministry whom we never saw again. We have no idea what became of them. They have sought ordination in our church here so they could say, "I was set aside to the gospel ministry in the great First Baptist Church of Dallas." All of that is a contradiction to the plain word of God which clearly admonishes, "Lay hands suddenly, hastily, on no man." The candidate for ordination is first to be tried and tested.

There is a second clause that is puzzling, ". . . neither be partaker of other men's sins." What does that mean?

When a church ordains a deacon or a preacher, it is thereby placing its imprimatur on that man's life and its seal of approval upon what he does. The ordaining church becomes, therefore, a sharer in that man's work and ministry. If he leads people astray, we in the church have had a part in that deceptive leadership. If he teaches heresy, we have had a part in spreading that impure doctrine. If he does not faithfully perform his assignment, we share his guilt.

Some years ago I remember reading one of Augustine's prayers that amazed me. He said, "Oh, Lord, forgive me of other men's sins." That strange prayer is easily understood when you read this passage. I am not only guilty of my own sins, but I share the guilt of the sins of my children, of the sins of my church, and of the sins of my friends and my neighbors. My life is bound up with the family and the church and the community and the nation. I must accept my divinely assigned responsibility for helping guide all of these I know into the way and wisdom of the Lord.

Servanthood. The pastor and the deacon are to be servants of the Lord and of the people. One of the most emphatic of all the teachings of our Lord is this: "He that is greatest among you shall be your servant" (Matt. 23:11).

In 2 Corinthians the apostles are called deacons (*diakonos,* meaning "servant"). Thus, the apostles are "deacons" or "servants" of Christ. Several times, such as in Ephesians and Colossians, Paul refers to himself in this way: "I, Paul, a minister" *(diakonos)* or "I, Paul, a deacon [*diakonos*] of Jesus Christ."

In fact, I would not object to foot washing, the practice of the old Primitive Hardshell Baptists. It is not an ordinance, but it is a sign of the humility of the ordained messenger and officer of Christ. We are servants. Let the one who would be the greatest among us be aware that he must minister to us all. Even as our Lord said, He came not to be ministered unto but to minister and to be a servant (Matt. 20:28).

Rewards. Boldness in the faith is very apparent. If a man is a faithful deacon, he is not ashamed or hesitant to speak for his Lord or to say a good word for Jesus anywhere, anytime, to anyone. Those who lead the church have a special reward.

> For they that have used the office of the deacon well purchase to themselves a good degree, and great boldness in the faith which is in Christ Jesus (1 Tim. 3:13).

Never was I more disappointed than when I was talking with a Dallas businessman about one of the deacons in our church. The businessman said, "I did not know he was a member of your church." I replied, "He is not only a member of our church, but he is also a deacon in our church." "Well," he said, "I have been doing business with that man continuously for more than twenty years, and I never knew that he was a Christian nor that he belonged to your church, and I certainly never guessed that he was a deacon." A man who is faithful in that office is bold in the faith. He would not hesitate to talk to anybody about the Lord.

For more than fifty-four years, I have been a pastor, and I have never yet experienced resentment from a man because I talked to him about the Lord. Sometimes the man is a stranger; sometimes he is an infidel. But no one has resented my interest in his soul. If you have great boldness in the faith, God will help you. That is one of the rewards to the ordained officers of the church.

"They purchase to themselves a good degree. . . ." These words refer to the reward here in this life. There is honor and esteem and appreciation and love for a man of God who magnifies the office of a deacon/servant.

However, it is also talking about the world to come. There are degrees in heaven. Do not ever persuade yourself that heaven is a bland, blanket unanimity and uniformity of everything. It is not so. There are people who will barely get in to whom heaven will be like the highest grade of hell.

> For other foundation can no man lay than that is laid, which is Jesus Christ.
> Now if any man build upon this foundation gold, silver, precious stones, wood, hay stubble;
> Every man's work shall be made manifest: for the day shall declare it, because it shall be revealed by fire; and the fire shall try every man's work of what sort it is.
> If any man's work abide which he hath built thereupon, he shall receive a reward.
> If any man's work shall be burned, he shall suffer loss; but he himself shall be saved; yet so as by fire (1 Cor. 3:11–15).

If what you have built is wood, hay, and stubble, it will be burned up, though you yourself will be saved as if by fire. It is as though you ran out of the house naked with no possessions.

Surely, I do not want to be that way. There are rewards in heaven. The Lord speaks often of the rewards He has in store for those who work in love for Him. We are to forsake all and follow Him; and if we do, God has an eternal reward in heaven for us.

Peter speaks of the reward of a pastor:

> And when the chief Shepherd shall appear, ye shall receive a crown of glory that fadeth not away (1 Pet. 5:4).

Five crowns are mentioned in the Bible: (1) the victor's crown (1 Cor. 9:25), (2) the soulwinner's crown (1 Thess. 2:19), (3) the advent crown for those who look for His coming (2 Tim. 4:8), (4) the martyr's crown (Jas. 1:12), and (5) the pastor's crown (1Pet. 5:4). God has a special reward in heaven for the pastor who is faithful in his work. What a beautiful prospect that God would thus honor His faithful undershepherd!

What Is Unique to Each

Now we are going to speak of the unique assignments of each one of those consecrated, ordained, set-aside officers of the church.

Three words are used in the New Testament to describe the pastor. These words are used interchangeably. He is called an "elder" *(presbuteros),* a "bishop" *(episkopos),* a "pastor" or "shepherd" *(poimēn).* All refer to the same man. For example, Paul says:

> For this cause left I thee in Crete, that thou shouldest set in order the things that are wanting, and ordain elders in every city, as I had appointed thee:
> If any be blameless, the husband of one wife, having faithful children not accused of riot or unruly.
> For a bishop must be blameless, as the steward of God; not self-willed, not soon angry, not given to wine, no striker, not given to filthy lucre (Titus 1:5–7).

Paul uses the word "bishop" in the latter verse to describe the qualifications of a pastor.

The term "elder" *(presbuteros)* is actually the name for an older person. The patriarchs of the Old Covenant were greatly honored. The word "elder" describes the man who headed the family. There should be dignity for the pastor and reverence of the people for him. The pastor is also called a bishop (*episkopos*, a compound word with *epi* meaning "upon" and *skopos* meaning "to look over"), one who oversees the work of the Lord. He is also called a "shepherd" *(poimēn),* one who cares for the souls of the people.

Dr. Truett, the far-famed pastor and undershepherd of the great First Baptist Church of Dallas for forty-seven years, was greatly honored and deeply loved. When I came to the church, I was forty-three years younger than Dr. Truett, but I, as a pastor, inherited the same love and respect and reverence accorded Dr. Truett. Any church that loves and honors its pastor, whatever its size, is a wonderful church. The obverse of that is also true. Any church that looks upon its pastor as a hireling is a weak and unblessed church. There is no exception to that in the ecclesiastical world.

If a church wants to get rid of its pastor, let the church pray for him. God answers prayer. Pray for him, and he will become such a good pastor and preacher that some other church will call him and take him off their hands. It will work. To love and honor your pastor is the will of God. He is God's ordained leader in the church.

> Let the elders that rule well be counted worthy of double honor . . . (1 Tim. 5:17).

In Hebrews 13, the pastor is called three times the ruler of the church.

> Remember them which have the rule over you, who have spoken unto you the word of God: whose faith follow, considering the end of their conversation.
> Obey them that have the rule over you, and submit yourselves: for they watch for your souls, as they that must give account, that they may do it with joy, and not with grief: for that is unprofitable for you.
> Salute all them that have the rule over you, and all the saints . . . (vv. 7, 17, 24).

Look also in 1 Timothy.

> One that ruleth well his own house, having his children in subjection with all gravity;
> (For if a man know not how to rule his own house, how shall he take care of the church of God?) (3:4–5).

Paul says another thing about the pastor.

> Let the elders that rule well be counted worthy of double honor, especially they who labor in the word and doctrine.

For the scripture saith, THOU SHALT NOT MUZZLE THE OX THAT TREADETH
OUT THE CORN. And, THE LABORER IS WORTHY OF HIS REWARD (1 Tim.
5:17–18).

Paul describes the respect and reverence due the pastor as
"double honor." The first meaning of that phrase is stipend, that
which you pay somebody for something. The second meaning of
it is honor and esteem. To which of those meanings is Paul referring here? It is apparent, for he describes it in the next verse.

For the scripture saith, THOU SHALT NOT MUZZLE THE OX THAT TREADETH
OUT THE CORN. And, THE LABORER IS WORTHY OF HIS REWARD [*misthos,*
meaning "wages"] (v. 18).

If your pastor is a good preacher and pastor, he is to have
double his salary. Oh, I like that! I have told you again and again
that this is the inspired, infallible, inerrant word of God? I love the
Lord, and I like what He writes! It is just wonderful.

This officer is also called a "shepherd" *(poimēn).* In all of
my reading I do not know of a sentence that ever moved me
more than one I read in the life of Dr. Truett. While he was pastor
of the church in Dallas, he was asked to be president of Baylor
University. When the committee talked to him about leaving his
church and going to Baylor, he expressed in his refusal a sentence that has burned in my heart ever since. "I have sought and
found the shepherd's heart." And he stayed in the First Baptist
Church of Dallas as God's undershepherd for forty-seven years,
until he died.

My own experience is similar. I cannot remember, as far
back as my memory will take me into childhood, when I did not
want to be a pastor. As I look at the little children in our
Academy, I remember that when I was their age in elementary
school, I was studying hard to be a pastor. After having entered
the pastoral ministry, I was asked to be president of several universities and colleges. I was asked to be an executive leader in
the denomination, but there has never yet been anything said to
me that pulled me away from this desire and prayer and love of
being a pastor. If I resigned my church to be President of the
United States, I feel that I would be stepping down. If I resigned
my church to be Prime Minister of the British Empire, I feel I
would be stepping down. I love being a pastor.

When I was with my country and village churches, I was
single most of the time. I lived with the people. I ate with the

people. I slept in their homes. I knew everything about them. I loved them. I have only one objection to being a city pastor. I have never been in most of the homes of our people. I have never eaten with their children. I have never dealt with them and prayed with them in their homes. That is a great loss to me. I have never been in any home where I was not welcome, and I have invited myself into a thousand of them. I love being a pastor. I do not want to be anything else.

Regarding the deacon, we will consider only the historical origin of that office.

> And in those days, when the number of the disciples was multiplied, there arose a murmuring of the Grecians [Greek-speaking Hebrews] against the Hebrews [Aramaic-speaking Hebrews], because their widows were neglected in the daily ministration (Acts 6:1).

The Greek word *(goggusmos)* translated "murmuring" is an onomatopoetic word. It is a word that sounds like that which it identifies. Onomatopoetic words are interesting. A philological scholar will say that all of our words ultimately were onomatopoetic, imitating the sound of what they were describing. For example, "whippoorwill," "bob-white," and "cuckoo" are onomatopoetic words.

> Wherefore, brethren, look ye out among you seven men of honest report, full of the Holy Ghost and wisdom, whom we may appoint over this business (Acts 6:3).

The church wanted to choose men whom they might appoint over "this business" *(chreias)*. In the New Testament that word is used twenty-five times, and every time it means "needs." The deacon is brought into the house of our Lord to minister to the needs of the congregation.

We fall into all kinds of differences and troubles and problems, and those men, full of the Holy Spirit, full of faith, and full of wisdom, are to make the house of God a place of joy and gladness. One of those great deacons was Stephen—God's first martyr. It is wonderful to see laymen who are dedicated to the Lord and who love God just as much as any pastor or preacher who ever lived.

As a youth I was once in Washington, D.C., and listened to James L. Kraft, who at that time was head of the great Kraft food company. He said in his address, "I had rather be a layman in the Northshore Baptist Church in Chicago than to be head of the greatest corporation in America."

Some years later I preached in that Northshore Baptist Church in Chicago, and I was a guest in his home. There is no greater strength and witness in the world than a layman who is dedicated and consecrated to our Lord. Edgar A. Guest expressed it in this way:

> Leave it to the ministers,
>   And soon the church will die;
> Leave it to the women folk,
>   And some will pass it by;
> For the church is all that lifts us
>   From the coarse and selfish mob,
> And the church that is to prosper
>   Needs the laymen on the job.
> Now a layman has his business,
>   And a layman has his joys,
> But he also has the training
>   Of the little girls and boys;
> And I wonder how he'd like it
>   If there were no churches here
> And he had to rear his children
>   In a godless atmosphere.
> It's the church's special function
>   To uphold the finer things,
> To teach the way of living
>   From which all the noble springs;
> But the minister can't do it
>   Single-handed and alone,
> For the laymen of the country
>   Are the church's corner stone.
> When you see a church that's empty,
>   Tho' its doors are opened wide,
> It is not the church that's dying;
>   It's the laymen who have died;
> For it's not by song or sermon
>   That the church's work is done;
> It's the laymen of the country
>   Who for God must carry on.

They make an unbeatable team—a godly pastor and a consecrated layman. Put them together, and they will literally shake the world for Christ. They build to the glory of the Lord. May God bless our dear church, our laymen, and our laywomen, and may our young boys and girls who follow in our steps find the path that leads to heaven and to home.

11

The Difference Between the Kingdom and the Church

> He answered and said unto them, Because it is given unto you to know the mysteries of the kingdom of heaven, but to them [who do not believe] it is not given (Matt. 13:11).

When our Lord made the announcement of His kingdom and kingship, He met rejection and opposition. The kingdom then assumed the form of a mystery. It is in that form today and shall be to the end of this age. We are going to make a distinction according to the Word of God among these three entities: (1) the kingdom of God, (2) the kingdom of heaven, and (3) the church.

THE KINGDOM OF GOD

The kingdom of God is universal and eternal from the beginning to the end, all-inclusive yesterday, now, and forever. The kingdom of God involves and includes everything of God—time, which is a creation of God; matter, which is the whole universe above us and around us; the heavenly hosts and all the inhabitants of this earth. Everything God has created is a part of the kingdom of God.

> The LORD hath prepared his throne in the heavens; and his kingdom ruleth over all.
> Bless the LORD, ye his angels, that excel in strength, that do his commandments, hearkening unto the voice of his word.
> Bless the LORD, all ye his hosts; ye ministers of his, that do his pleasure.
> Bless the LORD, all his works in all places of his dominion: bless the LORD, O my soul (Ps. 103:19–22).

That is the kingdom of God—all of God's creation in all time through all eternity.

In 1 Corinthians 15, the apostle Paul says a true word about the workings of God, His providences, and His moving through all creation.

> Then cometh the end, when he shall have delivered up the kingdom to God, even the Father; when he shall have put down all rule and all authority and power.
> For he must reign, till he hath put all enemies under his feet.
> The last enemy that shall be destroyed is death (vv. 24–26).

Everything—the stars in their orbits, the suns in their courses, the seasons in their days, the generations in their passing, all time and history—moves toward the great consummation of the age when all of it shall be dissolved and absorbed into the kingdom of God. All creation, all history, the kingdom of heaven, the church, we on the earth, the angels of heaven—all one day shall be absorbed into and made a part of the final kingdom of God.

The kingdom of heaven is the mediatorial reign of Christ in this human generation, in this present age, in this dispensation. The kingdom of heaven is Christendom or wherever the influence of Christ reaches. All that has been done in extending the name of Christ is a part of the kingdom of heaven. It has to do with us in this world, with humanity and with mankind.

In it you will find everything. You will find wheat and tares; you will find good and bad; all of it is here together in the kingdom of heaven.

The church is an altogether different entity, separate and apart from all of the other creations of God. The church is the body of Christ. He is here on the earth, though invisible, in us.

> Give none offense, neither to the Jews, nor to the Gentiles, nor to the church of God (1 Cor. 10:32).

The Jew, the Gentile, and the church—those are the three tremendous entities in the word and providences of God in this dispensation.

In Revelation we read the story of the marriage of the Lamb.

> And I heard as it were the voice of a great multitude, and as the voice of many waters, and as the voice of mighty thunderings, saying, Alleluia: for the Lord God omnipotent reigneth.

106

> Let us be glad and rejoice, and give honor to him: for the marriage of the Lamb is come, and his wife hath made herself ready.
>
> And to her was granted that she should be arrayed in fine linen, clean and white: for the fine linen is the righteousness of saints (19:6–8).

How beautiful and honored is the position of the bride of Christ—His church. Beyond any description, she is exalted, honored, and glorified at the consummation of the age. There are other people at the marriage supper of the Lamb.

> And he saith unto me, Write, Blessed are they which are called unto the marriage supper of the Lamb . . . (Rev. 19:9).
>
> And both Jesus was called, and his disciples, to the marriage (John 2:2).

Jesus was not the bride; the disciples were the bride. They were called or invited to the wedding at Cana in Galilee.

When the church is presented to our Lord in all her glory, washed clean and white, there will be guests at the marriage supper of the Lamb. John the Baptist said,

> He that hath the bride is the bridegroom: but the friend of the bridegroom, which standeth and heareth him, rejoiceth greatly because of the bridegroom's voice: this my joy therefore is fulfilled.
>
> He must increase, but I must decrease (John 3:29–30).

John was not a member of the church. He died before Calvary. The church is signally honored and glorified as the bride of our Lord, and the rest of God's saints are the invited guests: Abraham, Isaac, Jacob, the patriarchs, the prophets—all of God's great servants who lived before the day of our Lord.

THE KINGDOM OF HEAVEN

> The same day went Jesus out of the house, and sat by the sea side.
>
> And great multitudes were gathered together unto him, so that he went into a ship, and sat; and the whole multitude stood on the shore.
>
> And he spake many things unto them in the parables, saying . . . (Matt 13:1–3).

There are four parables that Jesus taught the multitudes about the kingdom of heaven in its outward form, as human eyes look upon it.

> Then Jesus sent the multitude away, and went into the house:
> and his disciples came unto him saying . . . (Matt 13:36).

After He had taught the parables to the multitude He sent them away and went into the house and taught His disciples four parables about the kingdom of heaven from a divine point of view.

Therefore, the kingdom of heaven has an outward, observable appearance, and it also has an inward providence and meaning.

First, let us consider the outward appearance of the kingdom of heaven.

> . . . Behold, a sower went forth to sow;
> And when he sowed, some seeds fell by the way side, and the fowls came and devoured them up:
> Some fell upon stony places, where they had not much earth: and forthwith they sprung up, because they had no deepness of earth:
> And when the sun was up, they were scorched; and because they had no root, they withered away.
> And some fell among thorns; and the thorns sprung up, and choked them.
> But other fell into good ground, and brought forth fruit, some a hundredfold, some sixtyfold, some thirtyfold (Matt. 13:3–8).

That is the way the kingdom and the preaching of the gospel is received. Some people hear and they really hear, and they turn and are converted and saved and become members of the kingdom of heaven. But many of them do not hear, and those who do hear only hear for a moment. That is the reception of the kingdom of heaven and the preaching of the gospel in our day.

When I was a boy, every preacher I ever heard was a postmillennialist. They all were going "to preach in" the kingdom of God. The whole world was going to be converted under the power of the gospel. It is a wonderful idea but it is not in the Bible. Today it is a dead doctrine.

The Bible plainly teaches that there will be some who will listen to the word and then allow other interests to take their attention away. Some will listen for a moment but have no depth and then turn aside. For some, the cares of the world and the vanities, ambitions, and worldliness of life will take it away. But there will always be some who will listen. That is the assurance that I have in my heart when I faithfully preach the gospel. Not everybody will be saved; not everybody will respond; but God will always give us some.

In the almost forty years I have been pastor of the First Baptist Church of Dallas and preaching in this sacred place, there has never been a time when I have preached but that God has given us a harvest. It has never failed. I have that assurance from heaven. If I will be faithful, God will give me some—not everybody—but some.

There is a second thing about the kingdom of heaven from our point of view. In the parable of the wheat and the tares, the good man went forth and sowed good seed in his field. Then while he slept, his enemy came and sowed tares among the wheat. When it came up, Satan had oversown God's field. That is the kingdom of heaven as we look at it with our human eyes. It has been oversown by Satan.

Recently I listened to a family lamenting over their child. They had taught him faithfully through the years, but as a young man he had broken their hearts. Satan had oversown.

On the cover of *U.S. News & World Report* is a picture of Karl Marx with the headline "Marxism in United States Classrooms." The article says that in our universities and colleges there are more than 12,000 Marxist communist professors who have led a sharp turn away from the long-prevailing approach to American history—the story of American success. They are leading us to a bleaker new focus on inequality, alienation, and conflict. I cannot understand why these radical, left-wing, communist professors do not go to Russia. There is an open door from America to Russia, but nobody goes. But if you were to open the door from Russia to the United States, you would have so many millions of Russians wanting to leave that it would flood the world. It is the same in Cuba or any communist nation. That is why the communists built the Berlin Wall. The Eastern Germans by the millions were escaping the radical socialism of communism. There is no communist nation in the world that can feed itself. Communism is a dead, decadent system. It is the oversowing of Satan.

The third parable illustrating the kingdom of heaven is the parable of the mustard seed, which grows and becomes a big tree, in whose branches the birds of the air come and lodge. It has grown to have millions of branches, and on them every dirty, filthy bird takes its roost. That is how we see the kingdom of heaven and Christendom. You only need to read church history to see how much evil, corruption, violence, death, and persecution have characterized the church. Jesus says that we are not to be surprised.

Then look at the parable of the leaven. The kingdom of heaven is like leaven that a woman took and hid in some dough until it was all leaven. Leaven is a type for evil and sin. When a Jew observes Passover, he scours every part of the house; and then he looks up to God and says, "Oh, God, You being my witness, if there is leaven in my house, I do not know it. I have sought to scour it out."

The kingdom of heaven is like that. There is no section immune to it. You will find evil infiltrating the church, the school, the mission field—everywhere you will find the weakness of humanity and the oversowing of Satan.

Then the Lord took His disciples aside privately and taught them the inner secrets of the kingdom of heaven. First, the kingdom of heaven is like treasure hid in the field. That is Israel. Buried among the nations of the world are the chosen people of our Lord. God's people, His treasure, are hid in the nations of the world (Ezek. 37).

Of all the verses in the Bible, the passage most impossible for me to understand is found in Romans 11:

> And so all Israel shall be saved: as it is written, THERE SHALL COME OUT OF ZION THE DELIVERER, AND SHALL TURN AWAY UNGODLINESS FROM JACOB:
> FOR THIS IS MY COVENANT UNTO THEM, WHEN I SHALL TAKE AWAY THEIR SINS (vv. 26–27).

I do not know what that means, though I have studied it more than fifty years. All I know is that according to the Word of God, the Lord is never done with Israel—not in the past, not in the present, and not in the future.

Israel is a tiny land, not even as big as our metroplex. In one place it is only seven miles wide. It has no more population than our metroplex. There is not a day that passes but that this tiny country will be in a headline in Peking, Afghanistan, Iran, Egypt, London, New York, Dallas, Moscow—in the whole world. Whatever happens over there is the headline article of every newspaper in the world.

Israel is in the mind of God; it is in the mind of the world; and you cannot take it out. That is one of the amazing fulfillments of the prophecies of God. God has a great purpose for Israel.

The second mystery of the kingdom of heaven that He taught them privately is that the kingdom of heaven is like a merchant who in seeking valuable pearls found the pearl of great price and sold all that he had in order to buy it. We do not buy our salvation. Jesus did that for us. We receive our salvation as a free gift from His gracious hands. *He* did it! *He* bought it! *He* paid the price!

> For by grace are ye saved through faith; and that not of yourselves: it is the gift of God:
> Not of works lest any man should boast (Eph. 2:8–9).

It is something Jesus has done for me. I could not save myself. I could never be rich enough to buy my salvation; I could never be good enough to deserve it. Jesus bought us, and in His sight we are the pearl of great price for whom He gave His all.

In Revelation 21 we read of twelve gates—three gates on each side of the beautiful cubicle, the perfect New Jerusalem, our home in heaven. Each one of those gates is made out of a solid pearl. A pearl is the only jewel that is made by life. All the rest are made mechanically by impersonal natural law; for example, a diamond is made under intense heat and great pressure. On the other hand, a pearl is made by a wound, a trauma, a hurt. That is the way we enter heaven—in the trauma, in the hurt, in the wound, in the sufferings, in the tears, in the blood of our Savior. We are the pearl of great price, and we enter heaven through His atoning grace.

The third parable is the parable of the net. The kingdom of heaven is like a fisherman who casts his net into the sea. When it is full, he draws it to shore, and he keeps the good fish and throws away the bad. So it will be at the end of the age. There will be a great judgment and separation.

When I was a youth in southern Indiana, I went to a Baptist Association in which an old-time preacher delivered the sermon. I will never forget that man. His head was covered with hair white as snow. The theology of the old preacher was not quite right, as I understand the Word of God, but the spirit of what he said was so true. He said, "In the memorial services and the funerals that I hold, there will be a wife who will come and look into the casket on the still, silent face of her husband and say, 'Good-by, husband, good-by,' or a child will come and look at the still face of a parent and say, 'Good-by, mother, good-by.' That is not good-by. Good-by is the great judgment day when God separates the saved from the lost. Then will a husband say to his wife, 'Good-by, I will never see you again.' Or the wife will say to the husband, 'Good-by, dear, I will never see you again.' That is good-by," he said.

Though I do not think the saved and the lost will be in the same judgment, the spirit of what the old preacher says is true. There is a separation, a great gulf fixed between those who are in Abraham's bosom and those who are lifting up their eyes in torment. Together we are in the world, but there shall someday be a great separation. Lord, when that time comes, may you and I and mine and yours be God's, and may we have entrance into that kingdom of heaven!

The last parable is one concerning those who preach and teach, taking things out of the Old Covenant and out of the New Covenant and breaking the Bread of Life to those who listen. May God grant that the word that is preached and the message that is brought will always be in keeping with the truth of God.

THE CHURCH

The church is the body of Christ, the bride of Christ. She is "a called out" [*ekklēsia*] body in this world. She is beloved of the Lord. She is precious in His eyes.

If I lived one thousand generations, I would never be able to understand a man who says, "I want to be saved and I want to go to heaven, but I do not want to belong to any church." That is inexplicable to me. In heaven we are going to be with Jesus and with one another, we are going to sing the songs of Zion, and we are going to praise God and rejoice in His great goodness. How can a person look forward to being in heaven with God's people and to singing the praises of the Lord and to offering prayers of gratitude and glory to Jesus when he certainly did not like it down here. It does not make sense. The church is the beloved of the Lord—the body of Christ.

Soon after World War II, I attended a traumatic meeting of the Baptist church in Munich. As far as the eye could see the city lay in desolation and ruins. The bombs had destroyed both the city and the church. After the war was ended, the ragged, defeated, miserable, poverty-stricken little congregation of Baptists came together where the church building had been located. The preacher had been in the war and had been grievously wounded. He was crippled and walked with much difficulty. After the service, the congregation partook of the Lord's Supper; and after the Lord's Supper that little wretched group of refugees who had survived the awesome war joined hands and sang "Blest Be the Tie That Binds." The second stanza of that song simply melted my soul.

> We share our mutual woes,
> Our mutual burdens bear;
> And often for each other flows
> The sympathizing tear.

That is the fellowship of the church. If we belong to the household of faith, we care for each other, pray for each other, love each other, minister to each other. If there is any need within the body we ought to be there to fulfill it.

On occasion I talk to people who live miles away about coming here to our downtown church. One man said, "Pastor, that does not bother me. When we lived in Oklahoma I drove forty-eight miles to church. I loved it, and last Sunday when we drove down to your church, I felt that I had come home. It was just like my church in Oklahoma." I love that—a church where I feel I belong and where the people love me and welcome me. Nobody feels himself above or better than anybody else. We are all sinners saved by grace and love Jesus and His people.

Our assignment is to preach the gospel to every creature. We are to win souls to Jesus. We are to baptize them in the name of the triune God, and we are to teach them to observe the things God has given us to keep.

The apostle Peter, a great preacher, did that and baptized his converts. Philip, the deacon, did that and baptized his convert, the Ethiopian eunuch. We are to win people to Christ and lead them through the waters of the Jordan.

Last is the destiny of our church. It is to be raptured away. It is to be caught up into glory someday. Our Lord did not tell us when, but He surely emphasized the certainty of that glorious rapture in His word.

> For this we say unto you by the word of the Lord [Paul is emphasizing the fact that these are not his words but are from Jesus], that we which are alive and remain unto the coming of the Lord shall not prevent [precede] them which are asleep [they will see Jesus first].
>
> For the Lord himself shall descend from heaven with a shout, with the voice of the archangel, and with the trump of God: and the dead in Christ shall rise first:
>
> Then we which are alive and remain shall be caught up together with them in the clouds, to meet the Lord in the air: and so shall we ever be with the Lord (1 Thess. 4:15–17).

This marvelous passage in 1 Corinthians is one of the high-water marks of all revelation:

> Now this I say, brethren, that flesh and blood cannot inherit the kingdom of God; neither doth corruption inherit incorruption.
>
> Behold, I show you a mystery [*musterion,* a secret in God's heart]; We shall not all sleep [we will not all die], but we shall all be changed.
>
> In a moment, in the twinkling of an eye, at the last trump: for the trumpet shall sound, and the dead shall be raised incorruptible, and we shall be changed (15:50–52).

It would be glorious to live in that generation of His coming. The type of it is portrayed in Enoch who was walking along and suddenly was not because God took him. The type again is in Elijah as he crossed over the Jordan River and the whirlwind and chariot of God took him up to heaven. There is going to be a generation like that. The church is going to be raptured and taken out of the earth. What marvelous things God has in store for those who love Him!

Unworthy as I am and sinners as all of us are, we all want to be counted in that number with our names in the Book of Life. May the door into glory be opened to receive us forever in that better world that is yet to come!

12

The Final State of the Church

Like the recurring sound of a foghorn or a buoy on the ocean marking shoal or a reef, so are the repeated, reiterated words in the Bible regarding the apostasy of the church.

> Now the Spirit speaketh expressly, that in the latter times some shall depart from the faith, giving heed to seducing spirits, and docrtrines of devils (1 Tim 4:1).
>
> This know also, that in the last days perilous times shall come (2 Tim. 3:1).
>
> For the time will come when they will not endure sound doctrine; but after their own lusts shall they heap to themselves teachers, having itching ears;
> And they shall turn away their ears from the truth, and shall be turned unto fables (2 Tim. 4:3–4).
>
> Let no man deceive you by any means: for that day shall not come, except there come a falling away first, and that man of sin be revealed, the son of perdition (2 Thess. 2:3).
>
> For I know this, that after my departing shall grievous wolves enter in among you, not sparing the flock.
> Also of your own selves shall men arise, speaking perverse things, to draw away disciples after them (Acts 20:29–30).

These are just some of the passages that reiterate the prophecy of our Lord Jesus about the church of our day. Two thousand years ago the Lord spoke prophetically of our day, and what He said is reiterated by the Holy Spirit through the voice of the apostles. Our Lord said that the growth of Christendom and of the church would be like a tree starting from a small mustard seed and finally evolving into a big tree in whose branches every dirty and unclean bird would find a roost. He said it is like leaven, which in the Bible is a symbol of evil. Finally, the growth of that seductive evil will permeate all Christianity. That is one of the saddest things that anyone who is sensitively aware can observe in our modern day. There is no denomination, no faith, no communion that does not have the working of evil, a departing from the faith, and the renunciation of the great truths of the revelation of God.

In the Apocalypse, the Lord spoke to the seven churches of Asia who are representative of seven great developing stages in the history of Christendom. He begins with an address to the Church at Ephesus, "I have somewhat against thee, because thou hast left thy first love" (Rev. 2:4).

As that departure from the truth and the faith continues, He finally speaks to the seventh church at Laodicea. Here the Lord Jesus is on the outside, knocking at the door to gain entrance. The development of the church is more and more away from the great doctrinal foundations that are found in the Bible.

> Knowing this first, that there shall come in the last days, scoffers, walking after their own lusts,
> And saying, Where is the promise of his coming? for since the fathers fell asleep, all things continue as they were from the beginning of the creation (2 Pet. 3:3–4).

The sun rises in the evening and yet I do not see any sign of intervention from heaven. Consequently, losing the hope of the return of the Lord, the church finds herself at home in the world. The church, deceived by the caresses and tributes of the world, does not look for the return of her Lord any longer. She places the marriage supper of the Lamb in a far distant age so that there is no relevancy in life or prayer or in watchfulness for the coming of our Lord Jesus Christ.

Consequently there has developed in Christendom a new religion with a metaphysical conception of God, a new church with a philosophical conception of Christ, and a new interpretation of the universe with a pseudoscientific conception of matter.

We are going to look at the fulfillment of the prophecy of Christ and of the prophecy of the apostles concerning the church in this day and in our generation.

The Final State of the Church

There are several characteristics of the church of the apostasy that are very prominent. This church is based and founded upon natural law, not upon divine revelation. The supernatural is overruled in favor of observable phenomena.

In the modern church of the apostasy there is no personal God. God. is interpreted as merely the first cause or the prime mover or a great force of energy, but He is not somebody named Jehovah or Jesus. Consequently, there are no miracles or prayers. All that obtains is impersonal and inexorable law, and the church of the apostasy is founded upon observable, physical law.

This church is also characterized by a departure from the authority, the infallibility, and the inspiration of the Holy Scriptures. The Bible is looked upon as one of many divine efforts on the part of men to define God. There is not a revelation of God reaching down to seek man but rather a surge and effort of man reaching up to find the invisible forces that lie back of this physical universe.

There are evidences of that departure from the authority of the word of God everywhere. In Jerusalem, I looked at the seal of the Hebrew University. The verse used on that seal comes from the Bible.

> . . . for the earth shall be full of the knowledge of the LORD. as the waters cover the sea (Is. 11:9b).

Those words have the authority of the revelation of God in Holy Scripture. But when you read the seal of the Hebrew University, it says: "The earth shall be filled with knowledge." God is left out of it, and to my amazement many of the people in Israel are atheists—a most surprising development of life.

For generations and generations, this sentence was inscribed on the front of the City Hall of Glasgow, Scotland: "Let Glasgow flourish by the preaching of the Word." After World War II the city was rebuilt and they replaced that tremendous slogan of Christian preaching and proclamation of the gospel with these words: "Let Glasgow flourish," leaving off "by the preaching of the Word." There is a universal departure from the acceptance of the authority and infallibility and inerrancy and inspiration of this Holy Book.

There is also an attempt to define Christianity as being just one of many religions rather than the one true faith. I talked to an illustrious pastor and minister in New England. In describing his pulpit message and his church, he said, "We are above Christianity. We take what is truth in Christianity and what is truth in all the other religions of the world and amalgamate all of those truths, so that our church in its message is above Christianity." There is no better example of the church of the apostasy.

A CHURCH BASED UPON A DEIFIED HUMANITY

Not only is it a church built upon natural law, natural phenomenon, and observable development, but the modern church of the apostasy is also a church that deifies and exalts man and dethrones Christ. Its basic doctrine is that God is incarnate in all of us. The only difference between us and Christ is not in type but in degree. We also are incarnate God. All we need to do, according to this humanistic doctrine, is to fan the flame of deity that is in us. As we give ourselves to the progressive realization of our deity, we finally arrive at godhood even as Jesus was incarnate.

Not only that, but the doctrine says that mankind is under a dynamic law of evolution. Progressively, inexorably, necessarily, the law of the universe is that we have evolved upward and upward. There is no such thing in this doctrine as a perfection in the days past, a fall, and the need for a Redeemer. We are progressively reaching and rising upward so that finally we will be angels and maybe archangels.

That doctrine carries with it a strange interpretation of Christ. It avows that Christ Jesus of Nazareth will not forever stand as the perfect man, but we shall inevitably by the passing of generations progress and progress until finally we shall have a better Christ.

That doctrine, of course, would be annihilated and made ridiculous by the admission of perfection in the past. Consequently, there is no such thing as perfection in the creation of Adam and Eve. The doctrine demands that we must have evolved from the marsupial, from the anthropoid ape, from the simian. Such a doctrine would be annihilated by an admission that there was perfection in the past. All this doctrine knows in the past is bestial, animal ancestory, opening the way for our inevitable and evolutionary rising, until finally we shall have many Christs—many perfected men.

Their doctrine of sin is a corollary, a concomitant. It rejects our perfect creation by the hand of almighty God, followed by the fall into sin and resultant need for redemption. Their doctrine is that sin is nothing but a momentary, temporary obscuration of the sun, merely as dust upon the image of a coin, nothing but the drag of our animal ancestry from which we will evolve. Sin is nothing but our stumbling upward and onward and heavenward toward perfection. It deifies man and glorfies his evolutionary ascent. This is the apostasy of the modern church.

As though that were not enough, the church of the apostasy is characterized by and based upon social salvation. No longer is there any need for the gospel of the individual soul's redemption. The gospel in the church of the apostasy concerns the redemption of society by human efforts and means. Benevolent humanism is the new gospel. We achieve and attain salvation when we reconstruct society. Christian socialism is the kingdom of God. The kingdom of man replaces the kingdom of heaven. Our purpose in the church, in preaching and in all of the goals toward which we reach, is to remake society and restructure the social order.

The church of the apostasy would claim three great stages in the progress of humanity. The first stage would be theological—when men talked about, thought about, and wrote about God. The second stage would be anthropomorphical or anthropological—when men studied and wrote about men. The third and last is the golden stage of sociological, societal study of the structure of society, government, culture, and all the things that pertain to human life. In this third stage, we will have perfection, and the millennium and all things evil and dark and sinful and wrong will be legislated away as we restructure society.

This kind of doctrine maintains that there is no need for Jesus today. It suggests that Jesus was just one teacher out of a great succession of teachers and that we will have a better teacher in the days to come. Jesus was a child of His times and was limited by His own circumstances and culture. He was filled with messianic illusions which we, in this enlightened age, know are false and mistaken. And the modern church, according to the church of the apostasy, is gradually moving away from those messianic illusions. There is no need for preaching the redemptive message of Christ. His blood is like the blood of any other animal or any other man. There is no resurrection of the dead. There is no intercession of Christ in heaven. He has no ministry in the presence of the Father. He was a man like all other men; and when He died, the things for which He fought died with Him, and we are growing beyond the illusions that He entertained.

Here are six avowals which summarize the chief teachings of the Scriptures that are contradicted by the modern apostate church. It is the difference between God's revelation in His word and the modern church.

1. The Bible says that there is a personal God, the Creator of heaven and earth.

The church of the apostasy says that there is no personal God but an Eternal Energy or Force or First Cause. They reject the act of creation and claim that matter has always existed.

2. The Scriptures hold that besides man there are other created intelligences—angels, fallen angels, Satan. There is a kingdom of darkness under the rule of Satan, the fallen angel, the enemy of God and man, "The prince of this world."

The church of the apostasy holds that there are no angels whether good or evil, no demons, no Satan, and no kingdom of darkness. Even in one of our Baptist colleges an illustrious professor once expounded on the fact that there is no such person as Satan and no created fallen beings called demons.

3. The Scriptures maintain that man fell from his original perfection and goodness, coming under the law of sin and death, and thus needing a Redeemer—somebody to save him from the judgment of his sins.

The church of the apostasy maintains that man has never fallen and rather has evolved upward. It labels the first eleven chapters of Genesis as mythological or legendary. Regretfully, I would say that many of the theological professors in the world believe that the first eleven chapters of Genesis are tales or fables and that there is no actuality in them. They believe man has never fallen and that he never lived in the Garden of Eden. Therefore, he needs no redemption but is in the process of evolving into a state of highest goodness and wisdom. In time, he will evolve up to God Himself.

4. The Scriptures say that the only begotten Son of God

120

became man to redeem mankind from sin and death and that He did that on the cross. He is now in heaven as our High Priest, making intercession for us and preparing for the day of our coming.

Contrary to that, the church of the apostasy says that Jesus is but one of the sons of God, for God is incarnate alike in all men. Jesus is not our High Priest, for His work as a teacher was completed in giving us a moral ideal. He was merely a model for us, a man of His times. When He died, He died as any other man died.

5. The Scriptures declare that there is to be a kingdom of Christ set up at the return of our risen Lord, at which time His church, made like Him in resurrection life, shall reign with Him, and all the nations shall dwell in peace together during the millennium.

Contrary to that the church of the apostasy declares that there will be no return of Christ to the earth and no resurrection of the dead. Through processes of evolution, earth will see a perfected humanity and a new social order in which all evil will be cast away, and the kingdom of man shall come.

6. The Scriptures say that the conflict of good and evil between Christ and Satan will continue to its final climax in the personal triumph of Christ over Satan, at which time Satan shall be cast into the bottomless pit with those who follow him.

Contrary to that the Church of the apostasy teaches that there is no bottomless pit, no hell, no judgment, and no such contest between Christ and Satan, for all evil is but imperfect good, a stumbling upward, which will disappear as humanity inexorably develops.

One can easily see that there is a difference between night and day, between heaven and hell, between the true church and the church of the apostasy—the modern church. I see examples of that all the time. The World Council of Churches is mostly Marxist Communist. It gives God's money to terrorists and guerrillas who destroy families, take lives, and raid villages. They support such atrocities in the name of the coming kingdom of man.

The Bible is a book of prophecy. God knows tomorrow, and He describes it just as He describes the modern church. God has something to say about the destiny of that church of the apostasy.

In the seventeenth chapter of the Apocalypse, this apostate church is called "the scarlet woman," and she rides the beast. It is an amazing revelation to me. God destroys the beast. He destroys Babylon, the system of this evil world. He destroys the Antichrist. But, the beast himself destroys the "scarlet woman," i.e., the church of the apostasy. Weary of her pretensions, he turns and destroys the apostate church.

This apostate church carries in her own life the seeds of her destruction. She cannot live. The sentence of death is written upon her, and wherever in this earth you see a church of apostasy, she will be a dying witness. Her very atmosphere breathes of corruption and dead men's bones. She has no life and no power, no ability to save. She has no message except one of inevitable social progress which the world denies in every headline of every newspaper and in every chapter of every book of history in the earth.

The same Scriptures also reveal to us the destiny of the true church of Christ, the church of the faith, the church of the Book, the church of redemptive love. Her destiny, God says, is to be caught away, to be raptured to meet her Lord in the air, to sit down at the marriage supper of the Lamb, to break bread and to share the cup with our living present Savior.

Two will be in a field; one will be taken and the other left. Two will be grinding at a mill; one will be taken and the other left. Two will be sleeping in a bed; one will be taken and the other left. The destiny of the true church of Christ is to be caught away to meet God in the air, to find a home with our Lord in heaven.

This church is the "called out" [*ekklēsia*] family of the redeemed of God, the separated ones, the saved ones, the elect ones.

In the beginning Adam and Eve were elected above all the sentient creation of the world. Noah was elected; he was called above all the antediluvians. Abraham was called out from all the families of idolatry of the world. Israel or Jacob was elected above Esau and the Edomites. Judah was elected above all of his brethren. David was elected above all of the princes of Judah. Bethlehem was elected above all of the cities of Israel. Mary was elected above all of the daughters of Zion. The apostle Paul was elected above all the rabbis of the Diaspora and was chosen to be the ambassador of Christ to the Gentiles. And of the Gentiles, you have been elected to be a member of the family of God!

How can I thank God enough that I am not a heathen growing up in a place where father and mother and family and friend never knew the name of Christ. Why is it God chose me? How is it that I was born in a Christian home, grew up in a faithful church, and now pastor a Bible-believing congregation? Bless His name! I thank God that He wrote my name in the Book of Life. I pray that this same election and calling out reaches down to you to find repercussion in your life and heart.